FRESNO'S PAST

Erma Peirson
with Robert Peirson

Copyright © 2024 by Robert Peirson

All rights reserved.

Illustrated by Stepan Bybyk
Formatting provided by Trisha Fuentes

No part of this book may be reproduced in any form or by any electronic or mechanical means, including information storage and retrieval systems, without written permission from the author, except for the use of brief quotations in a book review.

ISBN:
979-8-9914131-0-7 (Paperback)
979-8-9914131-1-4 (Ebook)
979-8-9914131-2-1 (Hardcover)

*Dedicated to the families of James Marlow Peirson,
Doris Mae (Peirson) Dye and Wilfred Saams Peirson.*

Contents

Introduction ix

Prologue xiii

Chapter 1: A Great Valley 1

Chapter 2: Spanish-Mexican Regime 5

Chapter 3: Historic Fort 9

Chapter 4: Gold's Influence 17

Chapter 5: Early Settlements 21

Chapter 6: The Word Fresno 25

Chapter 7: Origin of a County 29

Chapter 8: The First County Seat 33

Chapter 9: A Pastoral Village 49

Chapter 10: The Elkhorn Story 53

Chapter 11: Water Comes to the Plains 57

Chapter 12: The Railroad Enters the Valley 61

Chapter 13: Time of Transition 65

Chapter 14: Growing Pains for Fresno 71

Chapter 15: An Important Election 75

Chapter 16: Eyes of Fortune 79

Chapter 17: The City on the Plains 85

Chapter 18: The Courthouse Site 91

Chapter 19: The Turn of the Tide 101

Chapter 20: The Eventual Year of 1875 105

Chapter 21: The New Courthouse 109

Chapter 22: The Lone Republican of Fresno County............... 115

Chapter 23: A Long Christmas Ago 119

Chapter 24: County Post Office in 1879 125

Chapter 25: First Schoolhouse 129

Chapter 26: The County Seats Incorporates...................... 133

Chapter 27: Land Bloom 137

Chapter 28: Sinks of Dry Creek 143

Chapter 29: Shelbyville Swindle 147

Chapter 30: Pioneer Physician 151

Chapter 31: Major Savage...................................... 155

Chapter 32: Railroads 171

Chapter 33: Fresno Land Grant 187

Chapter 34: Tollhouse and the Academy 191

Chapter 35: William Faymonville 197

Chapter 36: Early Religious Services 201

Chapter 37: Cattle Kings 207

Chapter 38: Jefferson James.................................... 211

Chapter 39: Henry Miller...................................... 215

Chapter 40: Fresno Scraper 221

Chapter 41: Frank Dusy 227

Chapter 42: Water Tower...................................... 231

Chapter 43: The Roeding Story 235

Chapter 44: M. Theo Kearney 241

Epilogue	253
Acknowledgements	257
About the Author	261
Historic Map of Fresno County	264

The Fresno Guide – Thurs., July 25, 1963

FRESNO'S PAST

By Erma Peirson, Researcher,
Fresno County Historical Society

Our Heritage

When this researcher was invited to undertake the mission of recording some of the incidents of Fresno County's past, it was to stress the importance of days gone by. This is needful else those memories that brought us to today may slip into the limbo of time. The past is important to a commonwealth. How otherwise can we perpetuate and evaluate the happenings, the causes, the communities, or the state that is the culmination of many decades of a changing series of events and countless persons.

For the sake of posterity, the Fresno County Historical Society strives to keep alive that past that brought us to our wonderful today in Fresno County; a county that has played a part in making our state THE first in the nation. The past must be kept alive in this generation to assure its memories in following generations.

We are an essential part of the result of manifest destiny, that conception which resulted in linking territories of the New World from sea to sea and became the United States of America. People traversed the wide expanse of the new land, over mountains and hills, across plains and deserts, crossing valleys and streams.

NO EASY TASK

This was no easy task, as all students and readers of the West know. The great westward trail was a time of travail. The meeting of the forces that culminated in California was not accomplished in a small space of minds of mankind

QUESTIONS POSED

Being the capital of World Agribusiness is a startling situation. Are we aware of the scope of it? Of its trends? Who in unfurling manifest destiny of more than a century ago was responsible for the triumph in Fresno County's share of the progress that is so overwhelmingly assured? Are we conscious of our greatness? Let us preserve the memories of our past, for they helped to make us what we are today.

Who set out the first vine? Who first experimented with the Biblical fig tree? Who saw the shape of things to come that would usher in the vast fields of cotton, of potatoes, of melons, of citrus and other diversified fruits? What landowners first realized the value of great fields of grain and planted the magnificent fields that produced extravaganda of green carpets and the rich, golden poppies that sneaked through lush blades? Who had the dream of vast hordes of grazing cattle? Who dreamed of the possibilities of irrigation in a waiting world?

There were tragedies along the royal road to Fresno County, but as no great feat is hewn out of weaknesses, and south?

What great names are etched on the scroll of Fresno County's history that have had far reaching results? Why did so many people come westward and chose this valley?

It was not always overcrowded communities, nor running away from personal affairs. Not in every case a state of economy. That restless, far-visioning horde of people, urged on by a mighty force, came.

Dr. Wallace Smith immortalized our valley by calling it the Garden of the Sun, and how right he was. There can be no garden without sun and heat and seasonal rains, or the winds that wave high and low to perfect the long, smooth valley and its high peaks.

Today we have water storage security and we are highly mechanized, but that does not alter our history one tinker's bit, for it is all the same — a great growth and expansion of people and growing things, homes and schools and churches.

FOR THE FUTURE

We are still growing in actuality and the purpose of the county historical society is to keep this alive in our generation and trust that today will unfold in tomorrow's archives of memory and record.

The Fresno Guide is the vehicle that will carry these recordings each Thursday.

We are hopeful that when attics and basements are cleared when old houses are

Introduction

Let's begin with a passage from Erma Peirson's 1970 book, *The Mojave River and Its Valley*, found in Chapter 12, Green Pastures of Victor Valley:

> Apple Valley is one of Victor Valley's components. It is shaped like a large bowl. Mountains on every horizon-curve surround it and there is a fine view in all directions except in times when the winds are gnashing and earth's smallest particles are lifted, obstructing the sight of the hills and mountains with yellow curtains. When one adult was bemoaning the fact that 'my mountains are gone,' a little four-year-old boy replied, 'Never mind, they are just covered with dirt.'"

That little boy was me.

I am one of twelve grandchildren to Erma "Marnie" Peirson. Her eldest grandchild, Trisha, was responsible for awarding Erma the nickname because she was unable to pronounce "Grandma" properly, and that was how it came out. It stuck and was a moniker that Erma enjoyed.

As she got older, she would rotate staying with her three children, including her son, Wilfred "Bill" Saams Peirson, who was my father. I have many memories of "Marnie" staying at our place with my dad, my mom (Donna Peirson), and my younger sisters, Susan and Julie. We knew her as a caring and nurturing grandmother. Unbeknownst to my sisters and me, this time in the 1960s and early 1970s was a productive time for her writing.

In 2016, our father passed away at the age of eighty-six. We moved our mom closer to where I live in Southern California. Among our parents' belongings were many boxes of family keepsakes. Susan and I worked with our mom and helped her put together two books, *The Donna Harris Years*, which covered her life before marriage, and *The Donna Peirson Years*, covering her married life.

From this research, I came across a box that had Life Magazines on top of it. I set it aside without investigating the contents. Later, I went to look at the box, and to my surprise, underneath a few magazines on top were our grandmother Erma's writings and research on Fresno's past.

It was like finding a time capsule. There were over forty newspaper clippings with the series of Fresno's Past articles along with some unpublished drafts. As we put together the timeline, there were at least thirty missing articles. After this discovery, I visited the Fresno main library and went through microfilm of almost three years of the Fresno Guide to recover the missing articles.

The next step was to use OCR to convert them to text so they could be assembled into the book that she had planned, carrying on her legacy. Susan and I spent nearly a year getting all the articles sorted and transferred.

I want to thank my sister, Susan (Peirson) Bates, for her support and consultation and all her hard work reviewing copy and doing additional research. We want to express our appreciation to Eileen Lucero for her support, advice and road trip research. We also want to thank our sister Julie (Peirson) Symons and our mom, Donna for their encouragement. Most of all, we want to express gratitude to our father, Bill Peirson, for saving her writings.

Illustrations from early day pictures and sketches were created by the very capable Stepan Bybyk. I appreciate his talent in capturing and bringing to life the historic structures and scenery.

A heartfelt thank you to Nicole G. for her outstanding copy editing as she worked to fact-check and fine-tune the wording to reflect current views of historic perspectives. For more in-depth history on the Indigenous peoples of the Fresno region, who are not the focus of this manuscript, readers may be interested in consulting texts such as David Treuer's *The Heartbeat of Wounded Knee*.

In the opening article to her Fresno's Past series, Erma Peirson wrote:

> The *Fresno Guide* is the vehicle that will carry these recordings each Thursday. We are hopeful that when attics and basements are cleared, when old houses are razed or moved, that many things that once had a livable value expressing something of the past of the county, they will be passed to the archives and exhibits of the county for preservation.

It appears that her vision has come true.

Enjoy,
Robert Peirson, 2024
Grandson of the author of Fresno's Past, Erma Peirson

Prologue

This researcher was invited to undertake the mission of recording some of the incidents of Fresno County's past, with the aspiration of stressing the importance of days gone by. Without this effort, those memories that brought us to today may slip into the limbo of time. The past is important to a commonwealth. How otherwise can we perpetuate and evaluate the happenings, the causes, the communities, or the state that is the culmination of many decades of events and countless people?

For the sake of posterity, the Fresno County Historical Society strives to keep alive that past that brought us to our wonderful today in Fresno County. The past must be kept alive in this generation to assure its memories in following generations.

We are part of the result of this expansion by European settlers that resulted in linking territories from sea to sea to become the United States of

America. European settlers traversed the wide expanse of the continent, over mountains and hills, across plains and deserts, crossing valleys and streams.

No Easy Task

This was no easy task, as all students and readers of the West know. The great westward settler trail was a time of travail. The meeting of the forces that culminated in California was not accomplished easily or in a short time, but was wrought from physical pain, hardships, dangers, month after month of tiring discomfort, the destruction of material belongings, of despair and of hope through time and tide and test.

Fresno, located in the center of the Golden state, now has world leadership in agriculture. Here at the portals of the western sea, it stands proudly on its own, a garden of Allah.

There is never an easy road to royalty. The paths that lead to and out from the summit of such a sphere are shaped by work, worry, and tribulations, but happily, always with a long-term vision.

We are living in a fast and ever-changing era and must keep our records clear. Where better than in the minds of mankind?

Questions Posed

Being the capital of World Agribusiness is a startling situation. Are we aware of the scope of it? Of its trends? Who, more than a century ago, was responsible for the triumph in Fresno County's share of the progress that is so overwhelmingly assured? Are we conscious of our greatness? Let us preserve the memories of our past, for they helped to make us what we are today.

Who set out the first vine? Who first experimented with the Biblical fig tree? Who saw the shape of things to come that would usher in the vast fields of cotton, potatoes, melons, citrus and other diversified fruits?

What landowners first realized the value of great fields of grain and planted the magnificent fields that produced extravaganza of green carpets and the rich, golden poppies that sneaked through lush blades? Who had the dream of vast hordes of grazing cattle? Who dreamed of the possibilities of irrigation in a waiting world?

There were tragedies along the royal road to Fresno County, but as no great feat is hewn out of weaknesses, there was also great strength of character in the pioneers of this valley.

Who Were They?

Who came to the great valley plains because of the urge of colonization that swept like a flooded, mighty river of humanity? Who came because of startling sunsets? Who walked through purple mists into a valley and found it good? From whence came the odd-sounding but abiding name of Fresno?

What forces pushed people into this inner kingdom of the sun, a pivoting point into the four winds—the fringes of desert, lost, austere, and magnificent; the mountains, beautiful and wild and abundant in resources; the mighty ocean replete with adventure and commerce; or to fair valleys to the north and south?

What notable names are etched on the scroll of Fresno County's history that have had far-reaching results? Why did so many settlers come westward and choose this valley?

It was not always overcrowded communities, nor running away from personal affairs. Not in every case a state of economy. That restless, far-visioning horde of people, urged on by a mighty force, came.

Dr. Wallace Smith immortalized our valley by calling it the Garden of the Sun, and how right he was. There can be no garden without sun and heat and seasonal rains, or the winds that wave high and low to perfect the long, smooth valley and its high peaks.

Today, we have water storage security, and we are highly mechanized, but that does not alter our history that continues—a great growth and expansion of people and growing things, homes and schools and churches.

For the Future

We are still growing. The purpose of the Fresno County Historical Society is to keep this growth alive in our generation and trust that today will unfold in tomorrow's archives of memory and record.

The Fresno Guide is the vehicle that will carry these recordings each Thursday. We are hopeful that when attics and basements are cleared, when old houses are razed or moved, that many items that once had value expressing something about the past of the county will be passed to the archives and exhibits of the county for preservation.

The administrator for the Kearney Mansion and the museum in Roeding Park with offices in Kearney Mansion, will treasure and evaluate every item of Fresno County's past that has history woven about it.

We are striving to garner the old, the forgotten, and the passing of history.

If you have come with us this far, please stay and help us to preserve Fresno's Past.

Chapter 1:
A Great Valley

Whatever touches upon the Great San Joaquin Valley will eventually find an echo in the name of Fresno. Conversely, there can be no history of Fresno County that does not become involved with the scope, stretches, and fringes of the vast valley that acknowledges Fresno as its focal point—its capital, let us say.

The first recorded history of the valley of undetermined size and boundaries, approximately a century ago, was made by Pedro Fages, who was a military explorer from Mexico and later fulfilled a governing capacity in California during the Spanish regime.

Members of the Franciscan order, followers of the order established by Francis of Assissi in the twelfth century, founded missions along the western coastal area and provided religious instruction to the native Indigenous people. No missions were established in the territory of what is now the San Joaquin Valley.

The delightful climate of the coast and the natural sea highway to Mexico made that area a natural locality for any settlements that might be made by native people or the new European possessors.

Less Accessible

The valley area was less accessible for settlement because of the lack of roads or trails and the high-walled mountains enclosing it.

The first residents of the Valley were the native Indigenous people, specifically the Yokuts and Miwok. In the eighteenth century, the European settlers were White renegades who deserted their military posts. Searching for deserters, Pedro Fages, a military leader, entered the valley in 1772. The renegades made no permanent settlements but subsisted by following the climate in search of generous wild food—grasses, fowl and animals.

Passers-by found no permanent interest in the wide, naturally fertile plains, so the trappers, fur traders and military surveyors passed on in their various trades and activities to become pathfinders throughout the West.

Fages, while not interested particularly in establishing settlements, found the Valley area and the mountain fringes a resource-rich opportunity to feed his garrison during a time of dire need for meat. Supplying them with bear meat, he earned the name of "The Bear" and aided in saving the few cattle of California for breeding purposes.

First Tour

In March 1772, Fages made his first tour into the Valley. His group was searching for the mouth of the San Joaquin River. Father Crespi, a journalist and religious core of the expedition, kept a diary, which was for many years the only recorded evidence of the exploration, until Fages' own journal was found in Boston.

The year 1772 is a key historical date in the annals of the San Joaquin's heartland. Two years later, Fages' history-making for the valley ended when, after a quarrel with Father Junipero Serra over mission-building, he was recalled to Mexico, where he served his king memorably.

It is interesting to note here some of the remarks that Fages made in his records of the Valley. His mention of the San Joaquin River was recorded under the name "San Francisco," having been so named by another Spanish military man, Jose Joaquin Moraga, whose activities we will discuss later. He described the people as good looking, living on large rancherias and abounding in grain fields and fowl and animal life.

Left Heritage

Although the Spanish people failed to make permanent settlements in the Valley, they left behind a heritage of their traditions, their language in place names, and a background of rich literature.

Mention must be made here of the first White man to make scientific observations in the valley areas. Father Francisco Garces came northward from Sonora (in what is now Arizona) and did not pause to make settlements. He made history in his two-fold mission: religious conversion of locals and seeking new and shorter routes to Alta California's northern area. He left a remarkably detailed two-volume diary of his wanderings and discoveries, traversing much of the San Joaquin valley but coming no nearer Fresno County than Tulare Lake.

Another name of great significance in the forwarding of the Valley is that of Juan Bautista de Anza, who led many expeditions from Mexico to the northern part of California, looking for new and better routes and permanent settlement, although he, too, only skirted the northern fringes of the Valley.

The Valley has a human history preceding the Yokuts and Miwok Indigenous peoples who lived there when the first White men came. There is evidence recorded of an earlier group of people who lived in the Valley ten thousand years ago.

Chapter 2:
Spanish-Mexican Regime

One wonders, knowing the riches of natural resources in California in the years when it was first discovered by Europeans, why some of the interested European countries did not follow through on their opportunities to make of it the great land it is. Many of the first non-native adventurers were lettered men, although their knowledge of scientific facts was sparse.

England had a toehold with Drake's voyages along the Pacific coast. Russia, China, and Japan had opportunities.

At the time America was discovered, the Spaniards, in their search for the wealth of the Indies in the early 1500s, continued westward with their adventurous spirit. The result was the riches of Peru and Mexico (New Spain) and Spain becoming a world power.

A Rich History

There is a rich and exciting history in the tale of the Seven Golden Cities of Cibola, the kingdom of Quivera, Ponce de Leon's fountain of youth and the wealth of beautiful Spanish names.

Had the Spanish of later decades had such men as Cortes, Coronado, and others of the middle 16th century, they would have grown more powerful with the riches of the Mother Lode.

It was beneficial to a California of a later century that the Spanish people added the religious fervor and the pastoral way of living to their inroads to California.

They sought mission sites, and they penetrated the less accessible areas of mountains and the valleys between the mountains for runaway soldiers.

Because of soldiery and mission priests, the San Joaquin Valley was discovered and explored, and another century found a state and its political divisions. We find the beginnings of the current Fresno County long before California became a state in 1850.

Ancient Ford Crossed

An ancient ford on the San Joaquin River (now spanned by a highway and a railroad) was crossed by a cavalcade commanded by Gabriel Morago in 1810.

Morago was the greatest pathfinder of that day and was also known for battling Indigenous people. He had explored this region several years before when the river had been called Rio de San Francisco. He renamed the river in honor of his father, Jose Joaquin Morago, who had served under Captain Anza in the 1770s when he led the first colony to California and made a settlement at Monterey. Morago is an illustrious name in the annals of early California.

The Alta Californian settlers led a relatively peaceful and romantic existence during the Spanish period. When Mexico became independent of Spain, there were many changes and expansions politically.

New Spain, or Mexico, pulled away from the mother country. Mexico was now the name of the once Spanish province on the Pacific coast, although it was still called California. The southern republic was acknowledged but there was very little contact between Mexico and Alta California. Mexican governors came to rule. There was an inferior army on hand. There were many foreigners coming to the newly settled land, the majority being new Americans who were essential to establishing successful settlements. The missions began to fail in influence and physically became secular, as privately owned foreign trade picked up.

Ready for Republic

The Alta Californians stood ready to form their own republic. However, the southern and northern parts of the province could not agree. There were many "growing pains" in the feelings and actions of the people, even including animosity between the civil and the military forces.

Then John C. Fremon stepped in. An officer of the United States Army, Fremon announced the establishment of the California Republic. The "Bear Flag" revolt of 1846 was speedy.

Meanwhile, the United States and Mexico were at war, and the new California Republic became absorbed by the United States. In January 1847, a peace treaty was agreed upon; in February 1848, the peace treaty was signed, and the old Spanish province went under the American flag.

No Occupation

Though abounding in Spanish culture and traditions, name places, and names of illustrious priests, soldiers, community makers, romance and warfare, there was never occupation of the Valley by the Spaniards. The Valley was off the "beaten trail" of Spanish-American colonization. Historian Winchell called the Valley "the back country" of Spanish California.

Though John C. Fremont was not the first White man or soldier to traverse the Valley's length, he placed his name prominently in his written records that he faithfully sent back to Washington and to his wife, Jessie Benton Fremont. Jessie was voluble in her command of English, as was her husband; she is believed to have assisted him in preparing his records for publication.

He came into the picture in the Herndon area and attempted to cross the Sierras eastward. After failing, he escaped through the southern end by the Tehachapi mountains and over the continental divide.

It Took Gold

Though events came thick and fast in California, finding gold in January 1848 was what brought the Valley into its own. Trappers, warriors, mountain men, renegades, gold seekers, empire builders, the clergy, the curious—until 1848 they all skirted the fringes or passed through the great Valley that could bide its time.

The libraries are well stocked with the stories of these people. We hope that readers, who want to know more of the past cultures that little by little added to the development of the San Joaquin region, will seek out the volumes of printed matter concerning these stories.

Chapter 3:
Historic Fort

When the San Joaquin trails began to bring thousands of European settlers through the valley, they experienced conflict with and threats from the Indigenous people who had existing communities in the area now known as Fresno County. Not only were the passing throngs in need of protection as they travelled to the gold fields to the north, but there were miners working the river area in the region that was to become Fresno County. There were also settlers who sustained trading posts and dabbled at small settlements along the riverbanks and foothills.

Keep in mind that at this time the region was a part of Mariposa County (later to share the vast area, for the beginning of several counties). There was some effort of protection for settlers from the County seat, which was first located at Agua Fria, and later at the city of Mariposa by the Mariposa Battalion, formed under orders of the state governor.

Later, troops were sent down from Benicia for a survey for a military outpost. In April 1851, Colonel G. W. Barbour arrived at a well-selected spot on the south bank of the San Joaquin River, and the erection of the fort was begun. First Lieutenant Tredwell Moore was in charge of the building activities. A rude log building housed the soldiers until more permanent buildings could be constructed. Colonel Barbour was a member of the United States

Indian Commission, which negotiated with the Indigenous peoples to create a treaty for a reservation, which ultimately was not honored by Congress but served to free up the land for the post to be built. This temporary fort was called Fort Barbour to honor Colonel G. W. Barbour.

Name Changed

When the fort proper was finished, it was named by Lt. Moore for Major Albert S. Miller who then commanded the Benicia Arsenal near San Francisco, the headquarters for the troops who built Fort Miller and was a West Point graduate of the Class of 1823.

Major Miller's career was an active and vigorous one. He had been involved in many important campaigns against Indigenous people—the Black Hawk War, in Seminole troubles, with frontier troubles, in the war with Mexico, and many notorious encounters. His promotions came from gallant and meritorious conduct. He died on December 7, 1852 at the age of forty-nine. An admiring junior officer, Lieutenant Treadwell Moore, who commanded the post, named the outpost for Miller.

The fort was built on an expansive flat, surrounded by oak and pine trees and a great lava mesa. Craggy slopes of granite and smooth, round hills made a pleasing background for the establishment.

Springtime

It was springtime and the wild California poppies filled the area with the rich golden hue that was a joy for memory and a thing of beauty as they shot up from the green wild grasses.

This site above the plains offered everything that was necessary for habitation: abundant timber, a stream of water for every use, space for building, and good soil for crops.

Logs were hand-hewn from the "digger pines." Materials for roofing and chinking were available in the right kinds of soil nearby. Building was started as soon as the conflicts with local Indigenous communities ended.

The frontier outpost was laid out on a level area, the bounds of the quadrangle being 350 feet from east to west and 200 feet from north to south.

Gravelly loams and clays were there to make the adobe walls, which were so popularly used in those early California days. There were at first no lumber mills. The special types of lumber needed had to be freighted in from Stockton. The white sand from the river was put to use.

Busy Troops

Thousands of blocks for the walls were needed, which kept the troops busy. Heavy wagons were used for the trips to Stockton for supplies and materials. Ox teams, eventually to be replaced by horses and mules, hauled the wagons. Tons of flat rocks went into the construction for foundations for the buildings.

The country was devoid of wagon roads, and the most favorable routes were selected by the drivers of the freight wagons. Natural contours of land, winding ravine bottoms, and even smooth, steep hills were followed—any possible stretch that would accommodate the high-wheeled freight wagons was used. At a later date, Fresno County Historian L. A. Winchell commented that "nature was the highway builder."

Fort Miller, established in 1851, was a quadrangle 350 by 200 feet, surrounded by a five-foot adobe wall capped by stone. This illustration was created from an original sketch made by C. F. Otto Skobel, a soldier garrisoned at Fort Miller in 1864, and a perspective drawing that appeared in an 1882 book by Wallace W. Elliot named "*History of Fresno County*". (S. Bybyk)

Progress Halted

At a point on the river (later to be called Converse's Ferry, today known as Friant) progress in routing was halted as the waters of the San Joaquin emerged in a rock-studded canyon. Steep, craggy hills allowed no wagon tracks, and it was necessary to grade the road, which was constructed along the northern bank of the river.

Except in times of low water, the first freight wagons were ferried across by improvised means. At the time of the establishment of the fort, the seasonal rains were over and freight labor made good progress.

In the first year's adventure of establishing Fort Miller, supplies were brought in by the overland route. During the June high waters of 1852, it was necessary for supplies to be sent to the outpost by a light-draft stern-wheel steamboat.

The route from Stockton was through a rough and tortuous channel that threaded its way through tule marshes to a landing place that became known as Sycamore Point. This spot is less than a mile from the site later known as Skaggs' Bridge. The first steamboat to use this method was fastened by cables to the sycamore trees from whence it got its name.

Cut Roadway

Later, it was found necessary to cut a roadway along the bluffs of the river on the south side of the fort. The labor was not difficult except at a jutting point of granite where blasting was imperative and large quantities of black powder were used. Dynamite was not available in those days. Over this roadbed were to pass thousands of people: prospectors and their burros, freight wagons, stages, buckboards and buggies; Chinese miners, White men, Indigenous people, and finally, automobiles.

The best of every type of material in the building of the fort was brought to the river installation. They brought redwood shingles, lime for plastering and mortar, coal for blacksmithing, shoes for mules and horses, and tools for craftsmen. Ammunition came with two howitzers, an artillery weapon similar to a cannon or mortar. Clothing for both military and civilian use was brought in. Flour came by the ton, and green coffee by the hundred-weight along with Mexican beans, fat, bacon, and ham for the officers.

Garrison Grew

As the materials were assembled, the garrison grew. Established by James Hulz and then operated by Alexander Ball, a sawmill in the sugar-pine belt of the Pine Ridge district at Corlew Meadow made lumber more easily available.

Placed at the highest practical point on the river, the fort was within easy access of the hill country beyond, and a trail was laid across the hills back of the quadrangle.

The fort was complete in every phase of construction. It had accommodations for a garrison of two cavalry troops or two batteries of artillery serving as infantry.

The fort's military career was brief and uneventful and was abandoned in 1858 when Fresno County was formed.

Fort Miller Blockhouse

The blockhouse that was constructed for temporary defense use had no nails in it. The logs were dovetailed and mortised. It stood outside the quadrangle.

For some reason not recorded in history, the small, crude building was left outside the military compound. One historian commented that Lt. Moore thought so little of the lowly blockhouse that it was left outside the quadrangle purposely. The buildings inside the compound were better made from granite, adobe and sun-dried bricks, and hand-cut lumber.

The blockhouse was used by the military for many purposes. Various loosely constructed buildings were erected between the blockhouse and the fort, and for a time the crude building did not look so lonely and lost as when first left outside the main fort.

When all the other buildings had fallen to ruin or had been razed, the venerable old blockhouse still stood, well-tested by time, utilized for various purposes, but never was there a hand raised to repair or care for it. It held its own, though, "with the pathos of unloved and neglected old age."

In 1954, a reconstructed blockhouse was relocated to Roeding Park. It was used as a museum of early Fresno County history and other exhibits. It stands as the oldest building in Fresno County. In 1996, it was dismantled again and given to the Table Mountain Rancheria tribe, which has land near the building's original Millerton location.

Sold at Auction

In 1866, the buildings were sold at auction. Judge Charles A. Hart, the first county judge after the formation of the county, purchased many of the buildings, including the old blockhouse. The blockhouse was used to house Judge Hart's farm animals. Many of the citizens also purchased units of the old military installation and lived in them.

For a long time, the property was known as the Fort Miller Ranch. Over the years, it increased in size. Judge Hart and his wife lived there until their old age, and after they passed, the property remained in their family.

Chapter 4:
Gold's Influence

According to a historian in 1933, "The San Joaquin Valley was entirely out of the pathway of the Spanish American advance." The area of the Gold Rush came only to the northern fringes of the then little-known Valley that stretched, long and narrow, between the Coast Range mountains to the west and the Sierra Nevada on the easterly side. At the southernmost tip, the Valley is shut in by the blending curves of these two ranges in what is known as the Tehachapis.

The Valley's history is much shorter and different than the California history-making of the missions, the Bear Flag Revolt, and the Gold Rush eras.

In fact, it was unpopulated until after statehood was realized in 1850. It was an uncharted highway to and from the gold mines of the north.

However, gold played its role in this high-grass country that flirted with the rolling hills at the bases of the mountains and hinted of treasures and allurements beyond.

A significant number of settlers stayed in the hill area along the San Joaquin River to mine and were rewarded, some richly, with the gold they sought. Merchants came to supply them, and there was an intercourse of commerce. Thus, settlements were started.

The Foundation

While some worked for only a short time before going on to new fields of activity, many remained to become the social and political foundation of the new Fresno County that would be sliced from the great mother of counties, Mariposa.

John C. Frémont, pathfinder and military surveyor and explorer, developed his property called Las Mariposa, which he had purchased during his exploring career in California. He sent a group of Sonorans under the leadership of the noted Alex Godey to work his property for him. He had long been confident his holdings would bring forth riches. Members of the Gabriel Moraga exploration group of 1806 had named the area Mariposa from the Spanish word meaning butterflies.

Frémont's success in the Agua Fria and Mariposa region sparked interest in the region for thousands of people, eventually leading to the establishment of Mariposa County.

Major Savage

In 1850, Major James D. Savage came upon the scene in his variable career of soldiering, mill hand, and trader. He paid the many Indigenous people he employed with blankets, knives, and other items for gold they found. From his combined activities he became rich and influential.

Gold camps were scattered along the San Joaquin River. History points to Rootville, a mining camp on the San Joaquin River (later to become the site of Millerton) as the camp just following Savage's.

In the summer of 1851, Coarse Gold Gulch became a bustling mining camp. Friant Dam now covers the spot where the first placer mine (the Jenny Lind) was located. The original town of the present-day Friant started in the

1850s as a ferry crossing known as Converse Ferry, with a variety of names over the years before being named Friant in 1907.

Then the Flood

The sudden roaring and thundering of rushing waters that came on Christmas Eve in 1867 doomed Millerton. The next day, there was little left of the town that had served as Fresno County's first county seat.

The gold was playing out, anyway, and the county was to have new interests in a new place.

It had boomed, like any mining town. Workers were paid in gold dust. Silver was scorned. Many thousands of dollars in virgin metal poured into the town. All the bars and gravel banks along the river had been gold-bearing. For forty miles of the river course of the San Joaquin, such places as Sulphur Spring Bar, Cassady Bar, Arnold's Bar, Red Banks, and Temperance Flat, were making settlers rich.

Millions were taken from the river in five years.

Pointed the Way

The history-making events of early Fresno County is largely described by American nomenclature rather than by the Hispanic.

Gold was not the foundation of this central area, but it pointed the way for generations to come.

The area of the pioneer "Mother County" of Mariposa that now embraces Fresno County comprised a medley of features: the great plains, the flowing and lake-bound waters, timber, fine trails and passes, and recreation regions.

From out of the hustle and bustle, the confusion and assurance of going for what they were after, those passers-by laid a solid base for Fresno County.

Chapter 5:
Early Settlements

As California was becoming a state, the territory now known as Fresno County was also experiencing growing pains. In 1850 it belonged to Mariposa, which became a county in that year; it was the 27th county in the state.

Major James D. Savage, the first settler of any permanency in the region, established several trading posts, or stores. Some of the sites are now included in Fresno County. In a colorful and rugged career in the San Joaquin Valley and its adjacent areas, Savage performed many services to settlers and to the government. He was influential with many of the Indigenous tribes.

In the early 1850s, three small settlements were started in the Fresno territory. They flourished briefly before fading into memory and are recorded on some ancient maps of the great California plains area.

One of these settlements was Kingston, located on the south bank of the Kings River, a few miles from present day Laton. Kingston was a stage stop for the Butterfield Stages at the only ferry over the Kings River. While it lasted, the town thrived. In 1858 it became a relay station for the Overland Stage Route.

Carved from Grant

This community was carved from the old Laguna De Tache land grant made by the Mexican government at Monterey in 1846. The grant was confirmed by the United States Land Office in 1853. An early settler to this region was Perry Phillips, who arrived in 1853 and purchased eighty acres of land at $3.50 an acre. He became a wealthy rancher and a prominent and prosperous landholder.

Millerton, named for the fort nearby, was originally called Rootville. There seems to be no decisive record of why the name was chosen for the bustling little town that was to become the first county seat of Fresno County and was finally destroyed by flood waters from the San Joaquin River.

In 1852, Ira Stroud and his family camped with miners near Rootville. Stroud decided to stay, and for a time worked in the mines, but eventually changed to running a saloon with a flourishing trade. Later the Strouds moved to Millerton with a number of others. The name was changed sometime in 1852.

The first town to bear the name of Fresno was Fresno City. Fresno City was built on the Fresno Slough, north of today's Tranquility. Stages made Fresno City a point of call. This area was part of the Jefferson James Ranch, which was established in about 1857.

Centerville Settled

Centerville, formerly known as Scottsburg (named for an early settler), was settled in 1853 in the river bottom of the Kings River. In 1868, the town was moved to the bluffs to escape flooding and at that time received the name of Centerville. Centerville vied for the site of the first county seat.

Firebaugh was another town whose roots went down in the early 1850s. Andrew Firebaugh was the first to settle, and the town bears his name. In 1854 he established and operated a ferry on the Butterfield Stage route.

Friant, originally settled in 1856, is now under water but retains the name in its new destiny as Friant Dam. It creeps into history as being the locale of the first placer mine in the county. This mine was called the "Jenny Lind" after the famous singer of that day.

Rich deposits of gold were found in the reef that crossed the river about three miles below Millerton. It is shown on early maps as Hamptonville.

Converse Flat

A license, the second issued in Fresno County, was granted to C. P. Converse to operate a ferry at Converse Flat, also called Jones Store, and sometimes spoken of as Jonesville. J. R. Jones was a general trader on the San Joaquin River. Later the area was called Pollasky, after lawyer and railroad president Marcus Pollasky, included the terminus of a branch railroad of Fresno. William R. Hampton, from whom the early name of Hamptonville was taken, was a merchant on the Fresno side of the river.

The first large reinforced concrete river bridge in the county was erected at the site to replace the old Jenny Lind Bridge, which had been washed away in a spring flood.

After 1907, the site became known as Friant. In the 1920s, the site was known to be named for Thomas Friant, a lumber company executive.

Lumbering, along with stock raising and mining, gave cause for the early town.

Tedious Operation

Permanent settlement of the Fresno territory of Mariposa County was a tedious operation. The only sections of the county that seemed to gather people were the regions along the riverbanks. The aridness of the vast plains frightened them, as did the ruggedness of the Sierra slopes. Conflicts with the Indigenous people also deterred the settlers due to safety concerns.

Until 1856, the territory was officially a part of Mariposa County. Settlement was necessarily slow, due to natural causes. It was scattered because the first settlers located in the mountain gulches and on streams where there was gold.

The population came mostly from a floating class of people who had little tendency to stay put. The territory was isolated and much of it remote from the seat of county government.

Chapter 6:
The Word Fresno

It is interesting to note that the first documental printing of the word "Fresno" was printed as it sounds: "Frezno." This appeared in the act of the legislature creating Fresno County in April 1856. "Frezno" was, and is, the ordinary American English pronunciation. The correct Spanish sounding of the word is a sharp "s." From then on, state documents used the Spanish spelling. However, there was never an act passed to correct the spelling of the original document.

The word comes from the Latin "fraximus" for ash. "Fresnillo," meaning little ash tree, is often used in Mexico and other parts of Latin America. Spanish and Mexican government groups passed through, but there is no record that any of them dropped the name.

"Fresno" was first used as a place name for the "Fresno River," which lies wholly in Madera County. The river was originally in Fresno County and lies wholly in the portion that was sliced off to make Madera County.

Santa Ana

The Fresno River was called "Santa Ana" by the Spanish California explorers. The name "Fresno" first came into use during the 1848-1849 Gold Rush.

When California, the greater part of the United States, and much of the whole world became conscious of the wealth to be found in the lower Sierra, gold seekers overran every place where gold could be found. Among the streams rich in gold was the Fresno River; many Spanish and Mexicans roamed the area in their search, leaving many Hispanic phrases with the Americans.

No particular episode happened to cause the name to be applied to the river. However, the name took hold and there are numerous stories handed down by early settlers concerning something about the "Fresno" plains.

Wild Horses

John Barker, a prominent early-day valley explorer and later a permanent resident of Kern County, settled in the Elkhorn area. He tells in a newspaper vignette of the "wild horses on the Fresno plains." These plains that were to form the valley floor of the new county when it was decreed were generally known as Fresno County, from the adjacency to the first Fresno City.

When the new county was formed, the name "Fresno" was an obvious choice. The older "Fresno City" was often spoken of as "Fresno City on the Slough." Before Fresno City was formed, use was made of the Fresno River, and the water-logged but fertile trough of the Valley was referred to as the "Fresno Slough."

Travel between Visalia (the first permanent town in the San Joaquin Valley) and San Francisco had to bypass the swamp country or be ferried across the streams. The road came through Pacheco Pass and followed the San Joaquin River to this spot called "Fresno Slough" where passing was made at a place that became the head of navigation of the Slough. This place became known as "Fresno City" (present-day Tranquility) and became well known.

Lively Community

This first "Fresno City" functioned as a lively community for over twenty years to fade out only when the new city was built in the area known as "Sinks of Dry Creek," which was mostly traversed by cattlemen who passed through the country.

When the railroad came through the sink area, it established "Fresno Station" there because it was a central spot in the county, and because it laid directly east from the "Fresno City" that existed.

The county seat was at Millerton, twenty-five miles away. The village decayed rapidly as soon as its riverbeds of gold were exhausted.

Fresno Station was advantageously placed within a few miles from an oasis in the (then) desert country. This green spot was A. Y. Easterby's ranch, established about the time the railroad was being laid and it showed what could be done with the area with water. A couple of years earlier, water had been brought to the farm from Kings River. This oasis is land that one now passes going to Sanger.

Railroad communication proved much better when compared to river shipping facilities, and "Fresno on the Slough" faded out, and "Fresno Station" grew to become the only "Fresno" in the Valley.

An important and long street in the city of Fresno also bears the ash tree name of "Fresno."

In approximately the 1920s, a San Francisco Bay steamer was named "Fresno" and functioned until the bay bridge was built.

The oddest use of the word "Fresno" is found in the scraper that came into use in the 70s and 80s for digging the first irrigation ditches in the county. A man by the name of James Porteous, who hailed from Scotland and came to Fresno in 1877, manufactured the scraper on a big scale. His plant developed into the Fresno Agricultural Works. The scrapers, or "fresnos," were shipped all over the world. The word for the scraper may be used without a capital "F."

Grew on Banks

The particular species of ash from which the word is derived is the *Faxinus oregona*. This tree, which is not so much a tree as a shrub, grew along the banks of the Fresno River.

One historian recorded that "the first big trees" were discovered by James Burney of Mariposa, later a sheriff, in company with several other men as they were hunting animals that the Indigenous people had taken in the area along the Fresno River.

These men reported the trees as "big" according to the record. Historian Walter describes them as "a shrub, graceful, but very noticeable."

Most historians agree that there is no known record of the reason for appellation of the name "Fresno."

Chapter 7:
Origin of a County

The growing pains for the formation of a county in the Great Plains country of the San Joaquin Valley began a few years after California was admitted to the Union in 1850. Mariposa, the 27th county of the state, and the largest of them all, to be known as the "Mother of Counties," comprised approximately one-sixth of the state, and included what is now Mariposa, Merced, Tulare, Madera, Fresno, Kings and Kern Counties, as well as portions of San Benito, San Bernardino, Mono, Inyo, and Los Angeles Counties.

This vast domain stretched from Tuolumne County to Los Angeles and San Diego Counties, and from the Coast Range on the west to the Nevada State line eastward.

Mariposa lost a significant portion of its territory to form Tulare County in 1852, and a bit more in 1855 to form Merced County.

Later, all of Madera County and parts of Tulare, Kings, San Benito Counties and small portions of Inyo and Mono Counties were taken from Fresno County territory.

Fresno County's own growing pains began about six years after the State of California and the County of Mariposa were formed.

Costly Travel

Conflicts with the Indigenous people prompted the establishment of a protective military post on the shores of the San Joaquin River where it emerges from the Sierra. This protection was needed for travelers passing through the valley and for the population of the mining camps.

Lumber interests, scattered stock ranches, the necessary mercantile establishments, and the military fort attracted a population that had many occasions and reasons for transacting business at the far away county seat of Mariposa County.

Travel was not only an expensive affair, but a tedious and lengthy trip, not to speak of the dangers along the way, such as steep and hazardous uncharted roads and wide, wild rivers to cross in times of high waters. Ferries and steamboat travel added to the expense of travel.

It was difficult for the mother county to do much in a tangible way to assist the settlers so far from the seat of county government.

Largest Center

Millerton had become an active community and was the most populous center in the region that was to become Fresno County.

Although there were valid reasons for the forming of a new county, political-minded citizens of Millerton with personal gains in mind had quite a hand in inducing the 1856 State Legislature to cut off the southern portion of Merced County, part of the mountain area of Mariposa County, and the most northerly part of Tulare County to form Fresno County.

On April 19, 1856, the people of Millerton, the most populous community in the region, petitioned the Legislature for the formation of a county. The creative enactment was made on May 26. At that time there was no other choice for a county seat than Millerton, which was not only the largest settlement but also the most active in the region.

The plains that were to form the floor of the new county had long been called "Fresno County," getting the designation from the old Fresno City on the Slough (near present-day Tranquility). It was a natural consequence that the new county also would bear the Spanish "ash tree" name. It was written on the petitioning document as "Frezno," but soon became "Fresno" in print.

Five Hundred

At the time of the formation of the county, it had only five hundred inhabitants and its area was much larger than it is today. In the 1860 Census, four years after its formation, Fresno County had a total population of 4,605, including the racial categories of White, "free colored" people, Asiatic people, and Indians.

After a number of carvings through the formative years to make, or to add to, other counties, Fresno County is still tremendous in size.

Soon after its organization, seven commissioners were appointed to arrange for county government. The first election of officers was held on June 9, 1856.

One of the first acts of the new county government was to build a jail. The jail was a flimsy structure and was of little use to the law officers. Certain types of prisoners were taken to Mariposa City for guarding.

During the first decade of the county, business was carried on in rented quarters.

Squatter Right

When the brick and granite courthouse and jail was built in 1867, it was erected on ground held by the county by squatter rights. The land was not surveyed until 1880, when the county seat had been moved and most of the people of the village had moved to the present county seat.

The town of Millerton (previously named Rootville) was never platted or incorporated.

Chapter 8:
The First County Seat

The citizens of Millerton pushed for the county seat of the new county of Fresno. It can also be assured that they had a hand in the changing of the location a couple of decades later to the new city of Fresno, which was to be located on the railroad line that came through San Joaquin Valley in the early 1870s.

The little mining settlement of Rootville seemed firmly entrenched, and the citizens, ever alert to the advancing of their fortunes, renamed the camp. Just as Fort Barbour, previously named for a member of the Indian Commission, lost its title to honor Major Albert Miller, the commandant at Benicia who was in charge of the establishment of a military protective post on the San Joaquin River, so Rootville gave way to honor the same man and was called "Millerton."

The little town that became the first seat of government in Fresno County eventually fell afoul of the raging river waters and lost its seat of power. The location now lies under the great lake that is key to the prosperous Fresno County of today.

Gold Discovered

Gold was discovered in the summer of 1852. The names of the four men who made the prospecting episode and discovery on the slatey reef that crosses the San Joaquin River about a mile below the townsite of Millerton have been preserved in the records. They were Jesse Morrow, William Bowers, Brigham James, and Theodore Strombeck. This rich claim became known as the "Jenny Lind."

As gold discoveries increased on the river, the European settler population grew. Not all who arrived came for gold; many came to engage in business pursuits. Professional men, merchants and mechanics settled to profit from the fruits of mining. Some were only transient, but many remained to carry on in the establishment of the brand-new county. History is rife with the names of many men who came to the hill town settlement, many following the seat of government elsewhere when its Millerton days faded into history's pages.

One early settler at Millerton was Hugh Carlin, who moved from the Fort and established a store in a brick building he constructed in 1853. This structure was the first of its kind in the county seat. Long after the town was abandoned, it stood as a lone companion to the large brick courthouse. It was razed in 1927, leaving only the county building as a memorial to the heyday of development and the link between the mining camp and a greater county seat.

Town Boomed

By the time the county was created and Millerton was chosen for its capital, the town had boomed. Saloons occupied the most promising spots. All types of gambling went on—faro, monte, and poker.

The "coin of the realm" at this time was gold dust, with few coins being in circulation. There were "slugs," gold formed in octagonal pieces, that were worth $50. Silver was scorned by the majority of people, although there was some floating about. The smallest denomination was the traditional "two bits" in Spanish or American money. Every dealer of any kind of business had his own gold scales. Thousands of dollars worth of the virgin metal poured into town. Nearly all of the settlers were prosperous.

This was the setting that the county took over: Millerton, one of the richest camps in the Southern Mines. It had its picturesque side in a time of unrestrained indulgence.

The Attire

> Historian E. C. Winchell recorded that the men of the day wore:
>
> red shirts, canvas breeches, slouch hats, high-topped heavy boots with nail shod soles in patterns hearts, diamonds, clubs, spades, stars, circles of squares — and the belt-hung pistol was the common apparel of the placer workers. Gamblers in fine raiment — black broadcloth coats and pantaloons, gaudy figured velvet vest, fluted white shirts, flowing ties, soft-skinned high-heeled boots, and hats of silk or fine fur. The Mexican or the Spaniard in his open jacket and slashed calzoneras, heavy, stiff sombrero, red sash or silver-studded belt; fine boots and his hidden dirk.

The historian's record goes into detail about the dress of the era and the mining camp. We read of the dandified "bar-keep" and his flashy clothes; the short-skirted senoritas; the petite Chinese women with their flowing clothes and dainty stitched and embroidered shoes; the buxom, barefoot Indigenous women; and the bamboo-hatted Chinamen.

We find word pictures of the trains of pack-mules and burros, the great freighting teams, the racing stage drivers as they brought their passengers into the main street, and always the busy rockers along the riverbanks, upstream and downstream.

True to Form

Life at Millerton, formerly little Rootville, ran true to form, no different than the larger camps of the era. Families moving to the area boosted the settler population.

Ira McCray was running a store up in Tuolumne County in 1853 and became involved in some trouble with the notorious bandit, Joaquin Murieta. To escape the dire fate that was threatened for those who denounced the bandit, McCray moved to Millerton. In the Cantua Hills of Western Fresno County is Murieta Rocks, which is named after the bandit due to being used as a hiding place by him and other bandits. Murieta met his end there.

McCray became one of the leading figures in Millerton. In partnership with George Rivercombe, he built a hotel and livery business that added to McCray's wealth he had brought to Millerton from the north.

McCray became a prominent man in county and town affairs after the county was created. He built a $15,000 hotel on the river shores. The hotel was the finest structure in Millerton except the courthouse and was built around an oak tree that had some sentiment for McCray. He also owned the first newspaper of the county, The Fresno Times. His activity and popularity lasted throughout the years of Millerton's affluence. However, his holdings were destroyed in the great flood that ruined Millerton. His last days were sad ones.

First Prisoner

Other names of interest and importance to the new county included Charles P. Converse, who established a ferry at a point on the river. He erected the courthouse and jail, and ironically became the first prisoner to occupy a cell when he was charged with murder for killing an assailant who attacked him, though he was later acquitted.

There was also Ira Stroud, who migrated West with his family and paused to rest near the Rootville camp in 1852. He stayed to work in the mines and later to run a saloon in Millerton. There were the Richards and Williams families who moved to Millerton with the Strouds. Later came James McKenzies and Hugh Carroll with their families from the fort. In 1855, Otto Froelich and George Grierson became pioneer merchants.

From the bustling little mining camp with its hey-day going full blast, Millerton soared into its historic day of a government seat, not ready for so heavy a duty, too full of the reckless, adventurous spirit of the times to ever get beyond the point of reaching for and receiving the power necessary to become an adult town. That would come later, some short distance away, where the railroad's coming caused a different type of town to rise.

County Jail

The building of a county jail for Fresno soon after it cut itself from Mother Mariposa's apron strings was symbolic of the time of violence and looseness among the early settlers and miners. It was logical, too, that the people and their county officials should soon start worrying about a courthouse. Although the county itself was not on a secure foundation until May 1878, the need and desire for the dignity of a government seat was uppermost in the minds of citizens and officials.

The looseness and slovenliness of the creative act that formed the county and defined its boundary lines caused a great deal of trouble during the first twelve years of its life.

There were land grabs to defeat, settlement for slices of territory for Merced and Tulare Counties, a county to turn loose (making Madera County a sort of third-generation twenty-seventh county of the state) before Fresno County came into maturity.

Echoed in Millerton

The looseness of the times was echoed in the town of Millerton, which started in its mining heyday when the citizens lived a "devil-may-care" type of living. This was carried over during the first years of its majority as a county seat.

For years the county carried on its business without an official seal, until February 1873 when one was adopted. Harry Dixon, the county clerk at the time, built up the design.

No records were kept in the supervisors' minutes of canvassers of election returns until 1862. There were no records of the county until many months later when there were casual references to the organization act in connection with boundary line surveys. Possibly this situation had to do with the fact that most of the people of early Millerton were "more competent to manipulate a shovel or a flail than a goosequill," as one early historian, Paul Vandor, stated.

Rented Buildings

Until a courthouse was provided, the officials of the county carried on the county's affairs in rented buildings, scattered in as many as four separate parts of the town. The rentals were renewed annually because there was always hope an official home for the county offices would emerge that year. The postponement was due to financial reasons, as well as a dearth of bids from building firms.

In 1859, Ira McCray offered his Oak Tree Hotel building at the price of $8,000 for a possible courthouse. The hotel was not purchased, but a decision was reached that plans would be secured, and a courthouse would be built. The matter rested there until November 1862, when plans were received, and a set was accepted. A site was bought by local residents.

Advertisements were placed in various papers in the settled communities of San Francisco, Mariposa, and Sacramento. A year later, after no bids had been received, the supervisors had the courthouse location fenced in.

Ads Paid Off

In 1866, the matter of the courthouse was revived and again advertisements were placed in the *Mariposa Free Press* and the *Visalia Times*. This time the newspaper ads paid off.

Charles Peck of Mariposa offered plans that were acceptable, and Charles P. Converse received the bid. An issue of $20,000 bonds at ten percent was authorized. Converse's bid was $17,008.25. Converse was awarded the contract under a $34,000 bond. Later, an additional amount was added to Converse's bid.

Construction began early the following winter, and the courthouse building was completed in the summer of 1867.

The building was substantially constructed but lacked designs of architectural beauty. Bricks were burnt locally, and granite was quarried from the fine rock below the town, near the river. Black powder was used to loosen the rock, and the fragments were hauled by oxen to the building site, where expert stone dressers fashioned the blocks by hand.

Hundreds of tons of rock were used for the floors, walls and inner portions of the jail. At the time, there was no jail in the state more secure than Millerton's.

No Celebration

A total expenditure of $24,336 was spent on the courthouse building. Even after the long length of time it took to get the building into existence, there was no celebration to mark its completion. No dedication. No laying of a cornerstone or buried records, names, or photographs.

In its short years of prominence, it served not only as a county seat of government, but its tribunal chamber was open to the citizenry as a town hall. All cultural events were held there; religious and political affairs were conducted, and lectures on the arts and sciences were permitted.

Balls and Receptions

Balls and receptions and meetings of fraternal groups rounded out the mission of the judges' chambers in the substantial court building.

The old "wooden hotel," rented for years as a courthouse, had been wide open for every happening that came to town. Records of the county were often carried in the clothes worn by the officials for want of filing niches, as there was no place for storage.

Millerton's Courthouse stood the time and tide of over seven decades, despite only eight years of formal service to the county. It was abandoned when the county seat moved to the new Fresno City on the railroad.

Millerton in the 1860s

Millerton slipped through its initiative years of the 1850s into a new decade that promised hope for a new and more profitable destiny. Men were focusing their minds on ranching, stock-raising, schools, better homes, new industries, and permanency. Mining was fading out of the picture. Stockmen were taking advantage of the tall, lush grasses of the wide plains for their cattle.

Ranchers were turning to waterways to make use of the great rivers that flowed down into the Valley. Canals were inching water onto lands that had been devoid of any water except from rainfall. The timber business flourished with the grading of the mountain trails.

Fort Miller, which had been idle for years, was reactivated in 1863. Rumors had been flying strongly over the territory that the citizens of Millerton were "rebels" and there was danger of "secession." Troops were sent down from

Millerton Courthouse and Court House Exchange buildings at the County Seat circa 1868. (S. Bybyk)

the north to settle the trouble only to find that the town was peaceful and law abiding, and the war scare was mainly talk.

In 1864, Ira McCray established Millerton's first newspaper, the Fresno Times, with Samuel Garrison as editor. Garrison was a rabid sympathizer of the Southern confederate cause and expressed his ideas rather strongly through the paper. He had practically been "run out" of Visalia formerly for those same views when he published a paper there. The Times was first published on January 28, 1865 and folded on April 5 after only ten issues.

McCray brought the first African American residents to Millerton. He employed Jane and Tom Dermon, with Jane working as a maid and Tom as a cook and manager in his hotel.

The great flood in December of 1867 was disastrous, and Millerton never recovered. The refreshing October rains came at frequent intervals and increased in volume in the November downpours.

As the San Joaquin River steadily grew in volume with the repeating rains, some of the businessmen began taking precautions with their merchandise, which was mainly stored in cellars. The rain fell without intermission into December.

Many Floods

There had been many previous floods; some strengthening of levees occurred over the years, which had averted some damage.

The Yule season of 1867 was upon the village, but the world of Millerton was gloomy and dismal as the downpour continued. Christmas Eve arrived with no feeling of the seasonal spirit. At nearly midnight, sudden crashing, roaring sounds awakened those who were sleeping and brought terror to the wakeful ones.

A high wall of water, rushing at an appalling speed, swept the region, carrying with it a massive, mighty tangle of uprooted trees from the mountains. This great ramming mass struck the village with a mighty force that nothing in the way could resist.

McCray's great oak tree around which his fine hotel was built was torn with its roots, and the buildings and the ferry boat went with it. The stone and brick in the hotel could not withstand the heaving mass. No buildings in the lowlands were spared.

Hopelessly Wrecked

Millerton was hopelessly wrecked. The bright hope of the previous decade was forever deferred. On Christmas morning, the sun shone through a bright sky that seemed like a mockery of the desolated village.

The rollicking, boisterous, and reckless mining town was ruined. Some of the citizens dealt with their sorrows in the damaged saloons; others met their troubles with courage and started plans to recoup. Others drifted.

Only six days after the flood, the townsfolk of Millerton decided to ban the Chinese residents from the town through the Chinese Exclusion Law.

McCray, once a leading figure in the town, could not stand up under his great losses. He left, broken in spirit as well as financially, to eventually die in the county hospital of the forthcoming new county seat.

The San Joaquin River that had made Millerton rich with its placers had come to be its undoing. The time of destiny was at hand.

Held Its Own

The fine new courthouse that had been so long materializing was one of the other few remaining structures. Built to last, it held its own. Water had come up to its steps only, and it towered over the ruins. The courthouse served as a county building for six more years before being abandoned.

It became the refuge of owls and bats and was desecrated by thieves and vandals. After standing idly by for many years waiting for the time when the waters would be secured by a modern dam and lake, it heard its death knell

It was destroyed not by the angry, raging waters, but by the hand of man. In spite of the aging elements of men and nature, it stood intact within its brick and granite structure until it was torn down in 1941 to keep it from inundation with the waters of Lake Millerton. The place where it stood is now under the waters of a lake, but still bears the old name of Millerton.

From the right bank of the San Joaquin River, the once rich mining town of Millerton had this appearance in 1870. The town then disappeared, submerged beneath the waters of the lake that bears its name. (S. Bybyk)

The End of Millerton

After the disastrous flood of 1867, many of Millerton's citizens held the same attitude that had carried them through the previous years: a sort of lassitude as though they realized that destiny was catching up with them after dogging their heels through the efforts to make a county seat out of the boisterous mining camp.

In 1869 the first suggestions for moving the county seat were voiced.

A fire that occurred on the evening of July 3, 1870 was another massive blow to the townspeople. On the previous day, a supply of fireworks had been received by stage from Stockton for the celebration of the Fourth. A group of men were together that evening when a question arose about the handling of the fireworks.

A man named McCarthy picked up a Roman candle and lit it. Sputterings from the candle fell on the pile of fireworks and, then and there, they had their fireworks.

The building burst into flames from the sputtering, crackling explosives. The fire spread to the big Henry Hotel, the Farmers' Exchange Saloon, Henry's livery stable and blacksmith shop across the street, destroying buildings and starting a fire on the roof of the new courthouse.

Started Hotel

Henry's losses amounted to $8,000. He overhauled the old wooden building that had served as the first courtroom and started another hotel, which continued in business as long as Millerton existed.

After the fire, the residents became apathetic. They complained that "everything was dead." There were no decent buildings left, no churches, and no society.

In 1871 the unrest became pronounced. There was talk about the railroad going into Fresno Station on Dry Creek.

The writing was on the wall. There were many business changes and dissolutions. The stage now took travelers to San Francisco straight through in twenty-four hours. This was considered swift transportation. The residents had an opportunity to see a bit of some other parts of the state and could compare localities.

Millerton, which had never been more than a straggling village, seemed predestined to never exist as a town.

Removal Election

The removal election was held in March 1874. Millerton had never had a town plat. In fact, there could not be a legal one in the face of the fact that it was "no man's land."

There never were any city officers. The county officers were the governing board. The land was unsurveyed government land of which no one could have ownership.

Despite this situation, buildings were erected, bought and sold, and leases were entered into. The courthouse site was included in this unorthodox situation.

Chinatown

Millerton had a Chinatown, which was the most populous section of the town. The residents lived in little one-story structures, mostly made of brick. Chinatown was the last remaining populated area in Millerton. One Chinese business leader, Ah Kitt, had a thriving blacksmith business in partnership with his friend and fellow blacksmith and deputy sheriff, Jefferson Shannon.

According to the Fresno County Historical Society, Tong Duck, also known as Sam Chee, made a business out of moving property of many Millerton citizens to Fresno. Lew Yick relocated his butcher shop from Millerton and later built a building in the 900 block of G Street that housed the Bow On Tong Association and its Kong Chow joss house. Tong Sing and Duck, who headed the Sam Yup Company, built a joss house on China Alley in 1889. Laundry owner Hi Loy Wong had a brick G Street building and taught Confucianism.

Before the railroad came into the valley, Millerton was on one of the seven eastern wagon roads that entered the state. This was the longest wagon road, going through the valley towards Fort Tejon and into the southern part of the state. It came to Millerton from Stockton.

No Official Name

Millerton's primary street never had an official name. It was called, variously, Main, Center, Stage, Water, River, and Front. In the dry seasons, this one street was a dusty path; in rainy weather, it was thick as "mud pudding."

One is compelled to wonder why the early settlers built their town on a riverbank instead of on higher ground that was better drained and away from the hazards of floods.

Doom really came on September 25, 1874, when the board meeting for the county supervisors was set for October 3 in Fresno. The last official removal act was transferring the inmates of the county hospital to Fresno.

After Otto Froelich moved his general store to the new county seat in 1872, there only remained two stores, one that carried staples and was operated by Chinese, and Jones' store, a couple of miles below the townsite, which carried a variety. The saloons were the last to break up.

One by One

Many families had moved to Fresno when the railroad came through to the valley. The hand of destiny was taking them one by one.

Millerton died, slowly but definitely. Everything movable went out with the population. Nearly all that was left of the White settler community were empty cellars and foundations. Chinese residents remained, and of course, the great county building.

The river, once called the San Francisco, flowed unfettered through many decades: sometimes angry, with water high and roaring; at times smooth and gliding down the water, course, icy cold, and crystal clear. The water sang a requiem for Millerton as it had been.

Chapter 9:
A Pastoral Village

On the Upper Kings River is a site that was once one of the largest settlements in Fresno County. It was the first town to develop on the Kings River. The settlement lay on the stage route between Stockton and Visalia and was the chief stage station on the Fresno plains. Throughout its existence, the settlement collected several names and changed its location after being initially established in the river bottomland. While it became the center of stock-raising, it also ranked well for its agricultural pursuits.

The site is today known as Centerville, although it is now not much more than a wide space near the highway with little semblance of its days of glory. The main highway out of Fresno to Kings Canyon and Sequoia National Parks passes by the historic site of many names.

The area was important enough to be a contender for the second county seat (although that did not seem to be a credential for candidacy for seeking such a post at the time). Fresno was only a whistle-stop on the new railroad through the Valley with scarcely any population other than the railroad crews, and Millerton was fast disintegrating. The fourth contender, Lisbon, was only a town mapped out on paper.

Rated Highly

In the Thompson Atlas of 1891, the little town was rated highly. A statement in the Atlas reads: "It is the centre of the citrus belt of the county and will always be a place of more or less importance."

The first name for the settlement was Scottsburg. This was chosen to honor William Y. Scott, the first sheriff of the county to serve out a full term in 1858-59. It was the first European settler town on the Kings River.

In 1882, says Paul Vandor, a historian of early Fresno, the town boasted eight hundred European settlers and three hundred Indigenous people on a reservation located near the town. It was then the center of population in the county, outrivaling Millerton and largely determining the county's politics.

In the beginning days, a ferry was the nucleus of the settlement. It was still known as Scottsburg when E. C. Winchell, the first superintendent of public schools of Fresno County, organized the Scottsburg district, along with one at Kingston, further down the river, and at Millerton on the San Joaquin River.

In 1870, its name was changed to Centerville.

The Town Grew

The town grew and flourished. Though it was repeatedly a victim of the winter floods, the residents did not give up, but courageously resettled and repaired the damage after each onslaught of the river.

It had all the ingredients that make up a small town—its school; a hotel with C. W. Caldwell as proprietor; a general store, owned by A. G. Anderson; the "Pegleg" Paden saloon; and other businesses. Its ferry was called Poole's.

When it was only ten years old, Scottsburg was not only a prosperous stock-raising community, but its political propensities were strong. During election campaigns when office seekers were going from precinct to precinct to make election talks, they made their strongest ones at Scottsburg, for as Scottsburg went, so usually went the county.

This building, the Centerville Hotel that sat on the bluffs, was the last building standing following the winter season floods along the Upper Kings River that would swell from bluff to bluff. Into the 1870s, as the town faded from existence, the building gradually disintegrated and disappeared. (S. Bybyk)

Although no lives were lost in the ravaging floods that came to the river bottomlands, the great flood of 1867-68 was disastrous. It is told that one prominent inhabitant of the town and his family spent one night in trees for safety while the waters rushed down the stream and over the land.

Siege of Malaria

This flood experience took the heart out of the Scottsburg people. Not only were they suffering the loss of their possessions, but there was a siege of malaria that affected their health and strength.

The stream won, and the population moved across to the high bluffs of the river area where it was dry and safer from the harassing waters every winter. With the move went everything that had been Scottsburg. As time passed, there was less thought given to the memory of the town's namesake. There were no records kept of the settlement's activities and affairs. Even the school district lost out as Scottsburg after the flood.

The faithful ones who stayed on the high bluffs realized the need for a name for their new settlement. It seemed that the settlers could not agree upon a new name. The new homes were scattered, some above the town, others below, and surrounding the area here and there. So, according to one record, it was agreed by all to call the settlement Centerville.

Petitioned Government

After the inhabitants of the bluff town had decided upon a name agreeable to everyone, they petitioned the United States government to give them a post office to be called Centerville. They received another shock. They were informed there was already a California post office by that name. They would have to choose another name.

The inhabitants were rather name weary. They had no interest in starting any more discussions that might become heated or tiresome.

They liked their river, even though it often treated them shabbily, and they looked to its name for a solution. Kingston was in use, and no one seemed to think of using "Kingsburg" as a name, though the separate town of Kingsburg had not yet materialized. They decided to call the river Kings River while the town itself remained known as Centerville.

William Hazelton was one of the first settlers in the Centerville region. He took up a quarter section of government land for cattle raising and added to his holdings until he had approximately seven thousand acres. With Harvey Akers and Jesse Morrow, he was the first to take water from the Kings River. His descendants have lived on portions of the original ranch for more than a hundred years.

For a while the town had the only church in the county.

With the rise of Sanger, Centerville conceded her place to that community; many residents moved to Sanger.

Chapter 10:
The Elkhorn Story

Elkhorn is a familiar name in the history of Fresno County. The name was first noted when the wide, grassy prairie-like stretches of the San Joaquin Valley was spoken of as the Fresno Plain. The area included land in the tule region, which ran for about forty miles between the Kings and San Joaquin Rivers.

In the early 1850s, John Barker, a young sea-roving Englishman who was already second officer on his ship by age eighteen, learned of the gold rush excitement in California and came to seek adventure and fortune. He found adventure but not much gold.

He was interested in stock raising and established a ranch near Kingston, now the Laton area. Although he was successful in Kingston, he had an adventure that caused him to settle in the tule region.

Virgin Country

The tules were thick, rank, and high, and because the area was hidden from the passing prospectors and travelers, John Barker found it undeveloped country.

In company with three other young men, he set out on an elk hunt. They followed the eastern edge of the tules that bordered Summit Lake and the several sloughs nearby.

Their outfit contained a wagon hauled by four gentle oxen that had served on such trips for so long they were easy to care for. When staked out or turned loose, they never strayed.

Each of the young men had a saddle horse along. They watched their horses carefully for fear of stampeding from wild horses.

The party made camp midway between the two rivers, selecting a spot close to a slough for the advantage of water. The water was satisfying to the animals, but to the men, it had an acrid taste. This came from the burned tules that were strewn thickly in the slough.

Still Dissatisfied

The next morning after their first camp they started preparations for a big elk hunt. By evening they were still dissatisfied with the taste of the drinking water and the next day started looking for a new camping site.

While he was trailing antelope, Barker found signs of water and returned to camp to talk to his friends about it. He asked them to remain in camp, and he took his tools and left for the water search.

His endeavors bore fruit. He found a low wide bowl-like depression in the earth and started digging. He finally struck impervious rock. When he hit the rock there was a hollow sound. Fearing it might be a cavern he was very careful, not wanting to risk falling into a deep hole. A final blow broke a large crevice in the wide, deep hole he had made. A stream of water gushed out and started to form a lake in the earth's depression.

Later Barker wrote: "The water was clear and cool, as fine as could be desired and as soft as rainwater."

Covered with Bones

The area about the tule location was covered with the bones of dead elk, bleached as white as snow. He made an immense pile of them to a height of about eight feet to serve as a marker of the area, as he knew he would be returning to it. The white pile could be seen for a mile in the uncharted country.

That site was to be called Elkhorn Springs.

The young men stayed at the campsite for four weeks, killing antelope and elk, which they dried and took to Millerton and sold to the miners and Indigenous people for fifty cents a pound.

Barker sold his Kingston property and re-established himself in the tule country. When the stage road was established from Visalia to Stockton, Barker opened a roadhouse to take care of the passing public. He found a need for food for the animals.

Barker hired Indigenous people to cut the wild grass to sell to the drivers of the supply wagons that went back and forth. He employed them until the whole tribe moved in. He ended up telling them to leave. He also employed the passing Mormon people who were on their way from San Bernardino to the Northern Mines.

Telegraph Line

The Butterfield Stage had a contract with the government to carry mail from San Francisco to St. Louis and Memphis in 1857. The route went by way of Pacheco Pass, Firebaugh, Elkhorn, Visalia, Ft. Tejon and Stockton, coming down from Millerton. Elkhorn Springs became a stage stop.

When a telegraph line was started on the stage route, Elkhorn was the wire terminal. The line was begun in 1858. Plans were to extend it from San Francisco to Los Angeles. The poles were hauled in wagons drawn by oxen. When winter came the hauling stopped. The mud was too soft from the rains to continue the work.

A telegraph operator was stationed at Elkhorn. News brought in by the stage was wired to San Francisco. News eastward was wired back to Elkhorn to be transferred by stage. The news sent eastward was delivered "somewhere in Missouri."

War Rumors

In the summer of 1859, war rumors made changes in the Elkhorn station. It was eventually changed to a northern route. During the three years that Elkhorn was a stage station, large sums of money were shipped for Wells Fargo. Gold bullion was transported for the rich Arizona mines and money was carried for merchants and the military posts.

In his memoirs, John Barker wrote there was never a holdup or an attempted one during the Civil War.

Chapter 11:
Water Comes to the Plains

Two powerful innovations—the advent of the railroad through the San Joaquin Valley and the successful experiments in channeling water from the Kings and San Joaquin Rivers for irrigation purposes—advanced settlement on the Fresno Plains. These factors, coming almost simultaneously, set the stage for a bright future for Fresno County.

Before 1860, no water had been brought to the land of the Fresno Plains. The waterless area was a vast desert. The sun beat down scorchingly in summer seasons and the winds blew wildly. Not until 1865 did anyone pause to make a settlement. In the early 1860s, W. S. Chapman and Isaac Friedlander bought from the United States Land Office an area of eighty thousand acres. From this purchase, various large acreages were resold, and improvements were made.

In 1865, William Helm came into the region with a band of two thousand sheep. He built a cabin in the trackless region, about six miles northeast of the present city of Fresno.

$1.80 Per Acre

A. Y. Easterby, who came from Napa, purchased about five thousand acres from Chapman and Friendlander, for which he paid $1.80 per acre. Purchasers of this land hoped to resell at the price of five dollars per acre.

It may be a disputed question as to who made the first attempt at farming. Whether Easterby was the first one or not, it is true he made the first successful attempt at farming on a big scale.

Pasture feed in the Napa country was, at that time, poor. Easterby gave Moses J. Church, a sheepman, permission to take his sheep to the Fresno Plains and let them browse on the Easterby tract of land. Church went to the valley for this purpose but decided to settle on government land in the hills along the Kings River.

Easterby hired Church, along with a man named McBride, to put in a crop of wheat on a portion of his land near Millerton. In this area, the alfalfa grew well, and sunflowers grew to a height of ten feet. The three men agreed that where that was possible, surely wheat would do well. They were right. However, though the seed germinated, lack of rain dried up the grain, and roaming cattle and horses finished off the crop.

Had a Dream

Easterby had a dream for his new land in the vast valley. He was a traveled man and had seen the orchards and vineyards along the Mediterranean, the grain fields of the ancient Nile Valley, and the rice paddies of India. He wanted to try what he had seen of irrigation in those countries on the Plains.

In 1870, Church and Easterby, with Frederick Roeding and Chapman, incorporated their interests and established the Fresno Canal and Irrigation Company.

Despite the crop failure in the Millerton hills, Easterby wanted to try a wheat crop again. He planned well. He contracted with Charles Lohse, a successful farmer of Contra Costa County, to plant the land with wheat.

He gave Church the job of irrigating. Lohse furnished the teams and labor. Easterby took care of furnishing seed, feed, and implements. He employed other men to haul supplies from Centerville, and lumber from the mountain sawmill. He built a house and other ranch buildings.

Planting Completed

By November 1871, Church had flooded two thousand acres. By February of 1872, the work of planting the wheat was completed. In April, supplies for fencing Easterby's four sections of land were received and an eight-mile fence was made, and the crop was safe from the roving cattle and wild horses.

In August and September Easterby shipped four million pounds (two thousand tons) of wheat to San Francisco, for which the railroad charged him seven dollars per ton for freighting.

Church, who was deservedly acclaimed as the "father of irrigation" of the county, was not the first to attempt to irrigate in the county but was the first to make an ambitious application of the method.

Because of his activities pushing canals and ditches through the area, Church was harassed greatly by the stockmen. Several attempts were made on his life. The passage in February 1874 of the "no-fence law," which specified that farmers were not obligated to fence their crops to protect their land from grazing cattle, ended the cattle war in favor of the farmers' interests. Many of the large owners disposed of their cattle or drove them out of the state. Free range in the Valley was past. Agriculture was taking over.

Colony System

Many new people were coming to the Valley. This was partly due to the colony system of settlement. It meant more and smaller farms.

Between the colonies, the canals and ditches weaving across the county's terrain, the railroad projecting into the Valley, and the seventeen post offices here and there in the county, the region was ripe for many things and events to come to pass.

Easterby and Church were not the only property owners to branch out and bring progress to Fresno County. Numerous fine ranches were being built up in the old "cow county," but they are notable because of the first successful attempt in irrigating a large holding. It was in such enterprises that Fresno County had its foundation on the road to becoming the world capital in agriculture.

Chapter 12:
The Railroad Enters the Valley

After two decades, Millerton was dying on the vine. Sycamore, later known as Herndon, held hopes of becoming a railroad town. Canals raced across the plains to distribute water to a parched and thirsty desert. Stagecoaches still swung into the main streets of frontier towns, unloaded their passengers and baggage and the all-important mail. Then they changed or rested the teams, exchanged the news of the times, and having added a bit of excitement to the settlers, cracked the long whips and dashed on to another "port of call."

Livery stables flourished, turning their domain over to the townsmen to gather for daily forums where they chewed over the problems of the valley, state, and nation. New settlements materialized. Mythical towns died before they were born on town plats. Ox teams no longer crossed the Sierra.

The cattle barons retired to the foothills or out of the state. The Golden Spike had driven in Utah and a railroad was pushing into the central valley of California.

In late November 1871, A. Y. Easterby's earliest sown wheat was growing vigorously. Two thousand acres of young wheat, spreading out in a bright carpet, more brilliantly green under the shining sun and clear winter skies, was a sight to see.

Stanford on Tour

Leland Stanford, one of the "Big Four" of railroad fame, was then making a tour of inspection of the rail lines into the valley. The rails had reached a spot in Dry Creek and a station had been scheduled there. Since this was the nearest rail stop to the old Fresno City on the Slough, which was slowly giving up the ghost and going back to the tules, the name was appropriated for the railroad station.

When Stanford's group reached the site, they heard of the big wheatfield and the method of getting water to it and went out three miles or so to see it. The great green land, an oasis in a desert and the first sight of greenness they had seen in the dry and dreary plains, amazed them. Stanford proclaimed, "Here we will build the town!"

Before they left Fresno Station, Stanford told the reception committee, "Gentlemen, this town can never go bankrupt with a fund like this to draw on." He was referring to the abundant waters of the Kings and San Joaquin Rivers, something like ten miles distant.

Arranged Sale

Quick to take advantage of a snap decision, the officials of the San Joaquin Valley land Association (which included Church and Easterby) arranged for the sale of 4,480 acres, including the town site, to the Contract and Finance Company, a subsidiary of the Central Pacific Railroad (later to be called the Southern Pacific). The town was staked out the next year when the word "station" was dropped from the title and a new town was born.

At that time, water was no closer to the townsite than the San Joaquin River and had to be brought to the working crew in tank cars.

A depot was built that was 60 by 120 feet in size. The town was staked out in April 1872 and platted in May. Upon the water problem lay the success of the town of Stanford's choice. What could he have seen in the sandy, parched, and dry land that seemed to stretch out into infinity? Was he prescient? Did he and his associates see a vision of growing fields, houses, and people upon the dreary plain? Was he able, as the English poet Blake wrote, "to see the world in a grain of sand?"

What of Sycamore?

And what of Sycamore, on the banks of the San Joaquin, where the railroad had also purchased four sections of land and planned a town?

Leaders of Sycamore, which had been located for the purposes of ferrying, steamboats, and proximity to water, had long been hopeful of a town. It had a commanding and picturesque location. It served as a construction camp for the railroad lines, and had been chosen by speculators, staked out and platted in the same year as Fresno Station. It had a post office and a telegraph station. The river flowed through tree-lined banks. The sycamore trees must have been abundant, possibly more so than the ash tree that gave the name of Fresno to the entire area, plains, county, two townsites, a river, and now a railway site.

Sycamore, too, had a long line of namesakes. It named a creek, mine, and a mission post. It had been Sycamore Point for a steamboat landing; it was on a wagon freight line to the county set. Now, it named a railroad crossing. What was in store for the town Sycamore, high on the bluffs of the great river, now that it had been abandoned by a corporation?

Gigantic Plan

A gigantic plan was made for the opening of the Upper San Joaquin Irrigation Company. History records the report that nearly three million dollars were put into the effort to make a great ditch, which only proved the ditch impractical. It had been designed to water two hundred and fifty thousand acres located to the west of the railroad. Extravagant plans were made for an eight hundred foot long dam to raise the water in the channel and a twenty-five foot long canal.

Because of the nature of the soil, the ditch banks would not hold, and the dam washed out repeatedly. When the Bank of America decided not to throw good money after bad, the project folded. To add insult to injury, the lovely-sounding name of Sycamore was changed to Herndon to honor a humble Irish section boss.

The big ditch might have been saved by cementing, but in those days, cement was an expensive import. Sycamore went into the graveyard of forgotten dreams.

Chapter 13:
Time of Transition

When Fresno Station gave way to the new Fresno City, it was as though a magnet had been placed to start a movement of settlers throughout certain parts of the country. Following the success of A. Y. Easterby's wheat field and Church's irrigation ditches, there was a great pulsation of development here and there across the plains, up in the mountain areas and along the valleys of the two important rivers, the San Joaquin and the Kings.

Fresno City had its railroad, and not much else to offer except for its central location.

Over in Merced County, Snelling, the county seat, had given way to the town of Merced, which was on the railroad. Down in Kern County, Havilah, a gold mining town, became the county seat in 1866. Havilah, so named because someone in the diggings remembered a biblical phrase "land of concerning the Havilah, where there is gold." In 1874, Havilah, too, was swapped for another town on the railroad, Bakersfield.

It took a little over two years for Millerton to be on the auction block. In the meantime, Fresno grew in houses, lots, and people. For a long time, though, it stayed a dusty, dirty, desolate area.

Slow to Buy

Despite the easy terms offered by the railroad company for Fresno town lots, people were slow to buy. The company went so far as to permit newcomers to squat on lots and improve them with the understanding they could pay for the property if and when they decided to stay permanently.

The company tried to make attractive offers to get the town off to a good start. But for a long time, Fresno was described as a "desolate and forlorn looking station."

In 1870, another newspaper was started in Millerton. The town had been without social media for five years since Garrison of the *Fresno Times* got his come-uppance and retired from the field of journalism.

This second news venture started with the publication of the *Weekly Expositor* on April 27. It was published on Wednesdays by Peters and Company, having been launched by J. W. Ferguson, a California pioneer who had come to the Valley from Yuba City. Peters retired from the firm in November 1871, and the firm became Ferguson and Heaton. A couple of years later, Heaton sold out to Ferguson.

Two Hundred Copies

The first issue of the *Expositor* ran off two hundred copies on a Washington hand press, hauled down from Stockton for a supposed rate of two cents per pound. However, the bill was figured at the rate of seven cents.

The newspaper plant was mortgaged to meet the expense and the shipper had to take part of his pay in advertising. Soon after the paper was settled, the owners were notified they must find other quarters. They moved the plant to a stable where the staff batched as there was not enough business to warrant life in a boarding house. They had to move again and found quarters in a carpenter's shop.

The *Expositor* kept up with the activities of the Valley. No weekly issue was without some sort of railroad news. In the February 28, 1872 edition, the

Expositor recorded: "The *Expositor* was informed that 2,000 laborers, white and Chinese, are constructing the road in the county," and prophesied that "the iron horse will be snorting and panting on the banks of the San Joaquin before the end of the month."

By April 24, the railroad track was completed sixteen miles south of the river. The workmen built sidetracks and turn tables at the "station on Dry Creek" (Fresno) and the *Expositor* wrote that "'it had not seen the spot yet," but was advised, "it is a desirable location."

First Write-up

The May 1st issue included the first write-up of new Fresno: "We learn that business is very lively in the railroad station on the San Joaquin River. Immense quantities of freight for different parts of the San Joaquin, Tulare and Kern valleys. Wood is pouring in at a lively rate and the number of teams which arrive and depart daily reminds one of the palmy days of teaming Stockton used to enjoy. The station is a railroad town in the strictest sense of the word. It abounds in tents, 'rot gut' and roughs."

Already there was beginning talk about moving the county seat. The *Expositor* came out on May 8 with an editorial on the subject: "The most prominent candidate for the honor at present is the embryo railroad town near the sinks of Big Dry Creek, dubbed 'Fresno City.' The location of this proposed town is the center of the finest agricultural land in the county, most of which is susceptible of irrigation from one of the branches of the Fresno Canal and Irrigation Company's ditch, besides being the outlet for Bib Creek Valley, one of the most prosperous farming regions."

'Highly Pleased'

In early June the *Expositor* reported a conversation with "several gentlemen" and said "they were highly pleased with the new townsite. The land for miles around is excellent, is as level as the floor, it is capable of being irrigated, water can be flown through the streets, ensuring the decoration of the town with handsome trees, shrubs and flowers and making it delightful and attractive."

Rivalry for the hoped-for future county seat was rearing its head in the spring of 1872. A two-column letter "from the pen of one of our heaviest taxpayers" made argument in favor of Centerville instead of Fresno for the county seat. The taxpayer wrote,

> Fresno Station has no claims on our people for making it the county seat, neither can it advocate a situation that promises to be permanent. On the west side of the track you find a barren desert, extending to Hawthorne Station: on the north side of said station towards the San Joaquin distance of fifteen miles is equally unproductive, while on the south side toward Kings River the entire route being dotted with drifted sand hills resembling India sands, not a settlement to be seen in either of the above directions, and if an experience of fifteen years residence in this region is of any benefit to predict the future, I predict that said deserts are likely to remain — then what is there that entitles said station as making it the capital city of our county?

Why distance the county seat in an open prairie without a tree nearer than twenty miles, depending on transporting fuel and trusting to a soulless corporation to bring to the settlers many delicacies that are now grown on our rich bottom lands?

Now 'Deserted'

By the end of July "all the railroad traders" who went forward with the railroad folded their tents and departed. None were left but actual settlers, and, according to the newspaper, "in consequence of which the town looks and is, deserted."

The paper made the prophecy, "Whatever progress it now makes will be permanent."

The post office came in September. They had been receiving mail at Millerton, sixteen miles distant, which first passed through Fresno City. Russell Fleming, stage driver and liveryman, became the first appointed postmaster of Fresno in 1872.

Reports were coming in that the plain on both sides of the railroad from Fresno was "alive with new settlers." Houses were going up. Farming was progressing. Settlers were "taking up" government land. The editor of the *Expositor* began publishing a real estate column because there were so many land transactions.

Cotton and corn were being planted. Drought threatened the crops, having a season with "nothing wetter than a heavy dew" until a five-inch rain fell Sunday, December 22. It rained again on December 24, and on Christmas Day.

Without a doubt, Fresno Town was on its way up!

Chapter 14:
Growing Pains for Fresno

Fresno City and Fresno County were in the throes of growth during 1873. The railroad was really something to brag about for both city and county. It was the measurement stick to win an argument about "where to settle." By that stick, the town grew despite the reality that it was not much more desirable as a place to live than when it had received its title of "Fresno Station" in 1872.

The railroad was bringing many newcomers to the valley. Those areas that protested Fresno's grip on being the main settlement of the plains were getting their share of new settlers too.

The whistle of a train, almost eerie in that bleak, limitless stretch of undeveloped territory, was a wonderful thing to happen in the hinterland. It gave promise of many things—more people, homes, farms, a means of obtaining commodities other than the bare necessities of life. It was an outlet, too, commercially. It had been said of the region that every want "from a pin to a gang plow" had to be provided.

No Silver Spoon

Truly, Fresno was not born with a silver spoon in its mouth. Its leaders were going to have to work for their place in the sun. Fresno would always have one big problem: water. For all the soil was a growing kind, it had to have water, as bread had to have yeast. The combination of Fresno soil and water was the "Open Sesame!" for the prosperity of the Fresno plains.

Throughout 1873, there was down-to-earth talk about moving the county seat. Millerton had become submerged in apathy. Business had become stagnant, revived only due to the infrequent sessions of court. The patronage of such persons as lawyers, judges, jurymen, witnesses, and others concerned with court matters was about all that kept Millerton in business.

To make matters worse for the county seat town, the State Legislature had passed drastic Sunday closing laws years before that were now being enforced with vigor. The law was intended for all places of business on that day and aimed especially at the saloons. History has it that Millerton bypassed the law. The gossip revealed that "Millerton was so far from Sacramento, that the statute was not long enough to reach!"

Encouraged Removal

The *Expositor* encouraged the removal of the county seat. Several localities presented claims to the supervisors, setting forth the advantages of the communities. The chief aspirants were Centerville, Borden, Big Creek, Sycamore, Fresno, and Lisbon, a town known only on paper. Millerton had its quota wanting to retain its heritage.

Almost from its beginning as a railroad station—a mere stop on the road—Fresno reached for its first star: to become the capital of the county. Fresno, that "happy accident" of a town, was on its way up from its inception.

In the sandy city, new businesses opened, one by one, as the months slipped by in 1873. Paul Vandor claims A. J. Maassen as the traditional first settler and businessman. He built himself a shanty near the railroad depot, dug a well, attached a trough, and started selling water to teamsters for their horses. He also furnished hay and added a restaurant and saloon.

Saloons, stores, hotels, livery stables, butcher shops, and professional offices came into existence.

Over in Millerton, the *Expositor* was keeping close tabs on the new town. It recorded new buildings and owners, as well as many a dance to celebrate the opening of new enterprises.

News Plentiful

News was so plentiful in August that the *Expositor* had a representative in Fresno City. Around that time, the term "Fresnoite" was first used in print.

July 4 was a day of grand celebration. The town was barely a year old and getting quite husky for such a youngster. The celebration was a "great success," according to the newspaper. There was a parade with George Zeis, a boot and shoe merchant, as marshal. There was singing, and the editor of the *Expositor* read the Declaration of Independence. "The poet of the day" read "An Invocation to Liberty" and Miss Lizzie Gilky impersonated the Goddess of Liberty.

Otto Froelich, a pioneer and merchant of the county at Millerton, saw the handwriting on the wall, and opened a store in Fresno in 1874, serving as the town's first "storekeeper," and later, its first banker.

Dotting the plains were numerous cabins of new settlers who were "taking up" government land.

Taxable Property

Vandor recorded in his book, *History of Fresno County Volume 1: The Early Days*, that the "county shows a greater increase in taxable property than any other in the state. Increase for the year was $1,291,412 or $814,972 more than any other county in the state and more property than Tulare and Kern combined."

In September 1873, the editor of the *Expositor*, who had been elected to the State Assembly, was married to Miss Agnes L. Lails of San Jose. Later that autumn, J. W. Ferguson and C. A. Heaton dissolved their partnership in the news plant.

Ferguson seems to have had a special position in Fresno County from the time he launched his news sheet in 1870 and on through the years. He watched through the keyhole, so to speak, until the time was ripe for bigger and better things in the way of progress for his adopted county.

Pendulum of Growth

He pioneered during the years he helped to swing the pendulum of growth and advancement there in old Millerton. When he saw the way that the wind was blowing county-seat wise, he jumped into the caldron of publicity, expansion, politics, and grassroots.

In his paper, he wrote, "honestly, the devil with them all!" He practically counted the heads of those who strayed from the straight and narrow paths. In the November 26, 1873 *Expositor* issue, he reported through his paper, "Only half a dozen drunken men were noticed in town," and commented further, "the moral tone of the place must be improving."

He used his influence through the pages of the *Expositor* to aid the famous No-Fence bill to protect agriculture and to prevent the trespassing of animals upon private property in the counties of Fresno, Tulare, and Kern.

Chapter 15:
An Important Election

It was a great day! Election day had arrived. The wishing and wanting, the working and the waiting, the protesting and the planning, the rivalry and the racketing—it was over. The "be-all and end-all" day set the stage for a new drama and a new era. Settlers had become U.S. citizens. The talk, the visions, the wondering would all be settled by the democratic way of life—the ballot.

On February 18, 1874, the board of supervisors ordered an election to decide on the removal of the county seat from Millerton and the "candidate" localities to be voted upon.

Before the date of the election, all localities except Fresno, Lisbon, Centerville and Millerton withdrew from consideration.

March 23 was election day. Seven hundred and fifty-seven votes were cast throughout the county.

The Winner

Three days after the election, the *Expositor* came out with an eleven-line headline to proclaim the results. Fresno had won, receiving 417 votes!

Of the 112 votes cast in Fresno, 111 were cast for Fresno as the county seat. The remaining lone vote had gone for Lisbon, which was only a plan for a town to be "located" on the banks of Big Dry Creek, five miles northeast of Clovis.

Even without residents to vote for it, Lisbon received second place with a total of 124 votes. The largest number of these votes came from residents of Big Dry Creek. Added to Dry Creek's fifty-four votes were forty-one from Yancy, a precinct on the Chowchilla River.

Millerton residents cast sixteen votes for Lisbon. There were eleven votes for it from Centerville. Buchanan, a settlement in the northern foothills, also contributed one vote for Lisbon.

Even with the encouragement of second place, Lisbon failed to materialize as a community. The place where it would have been was in Section 22, Township 12 South, Range 21 East. Lisbon offered thirty acres of land for public buildings to the county seat locale.

Centerville, an active rival of Fresno, "the city on the barren desert," drew one fewer vote than the mythical Lisbon. It received 101 votes from its own settlement, one from Millerton, nine from Kingston and twelve from what was then known as Squaw Valley.

An Inducement

Located on the Kings River, Centerville offered all necessary lots to go with the gift of a settled community. One of the arguments offered by Centerville for receiving the county seat was that if removal had to be for the county seat, it should be to a locality that would "never need moving again."

At that time there was a feeling that the county would be divided by the next Legislature and that the northern boundary of the southern county would be the San Joaquin River. That division came, but nineteen years later.

The residents of Millerton cast sixty-six votes, with thirty-nine going to their biggest rival, Fresno.

One of the sites offered for the county seat, should there be need for land, was from the chairman of the board of supervisors, Henry C. Daulton. Daulton offered a thousand acres from his great ranch in what is now Madera County.

Nearly two years after the City of Fresno was platted, it became the county seat in 1874.

Behind the Vote

Historian Vandor recorded: "It was the participation in the election of the railroad hands that carried the day. The section boss of the railroad was kept busy hustling voters to the polling place, and as an inducement to vote for Fresno tradition has it that whiskey was carried in buckets and ladled out in tin cups."

Millerton had met its doom. On September 9, the birthday of the state, the editor of the *Expositor* wrote, "The glories of Millerton have departed, and in a few days, it will live in name only. One-by-one the buildings are being torn down and moved to Fresno . . . And who knows where the end will be? Farewell, poor Millerton!"

The legal change was authorized by the Legislature. On March 27, Governor Newton Booth approved the act empowering the board of supervisors to establish the county seat of Fresno County and erect necessary buildings.

The historic mining town of Millerton was officially abandoned as the county seat of Fresno County on September 25, when the official archives were moved to Fresno. The first meeting of the board of supervisors at the new county seat was held in temporary quarters on October 5.

Fresno boomed, town lots sold briskly, and business and residence locators were numerous.

Last Edition

In April 1874 following the election, the *Expositor* brought out its last issue to be published in Millerton. It was number 52 of volume 4. The building that housed the editor, his family, and the printing office, was torn down and hauled to Fresno and hastily reassembled at the northeast corner of J (Van Ness) and Tulare streets. This move was expedited. The last issue of the paper was on April 15; the first one in Fresno was number 1, volume 5, on April 22.

Historian Winchell recorded the *Expositor's* move: "To assort, collect, pack, load onto wagons, transfer 25 miles over the roadless plains, unload, segregate the jumble of the fonts, presses, paper, inks and all the other paraphernalia of a country newspaper, and desperately, almost without intermission, set by hand the types for the coming edition, was a task as the publisher said, 'to move a printing office is no fool job.'"

The editor made this announcement: "In our field at Millerton, we labored under serious disadvantages. The town was dead. The population of the county was small, and in some localities a prejudice existed against anything that smacked of progression, and in consequence the '*Expositor*', from its inception, has had the enmity of the faction. They promised, and rightly, too, that its publication would induce immigration and turn the fertile plains from a vast range to numberless thrifty farms . . . and we have done much toward inducing immigration hitherward, thus adding to its wealth and prosperity. In our new home, we find things different. The town of Fresno is growing and prosperous. Farms are scattered over the county."

Fresno County had a new lodestar. All seemed well with its world.

Chapter 16:
Eyes of Fortune

From the very beginning of Fresno City, the eyes of businessmen were upon her. When the railroad started permanent improvements at the site in the "Sinks of Dry Creek" back in April 1872, rails had been laid to the future town. Gang headquarters were in box cars standing at the new location site.

All about were the naked plains, with no sign of habitation except the box cars and their tenants. At Sycamore, ten miles away on the south side of the San Joaquin River, there also was a lively camp. There, traders in goods and liquor had set up several businesses, fully expecting the railroad magnates to locate their principal town in the area there.

Rumors changed their tactics; Fresno Station was the new favorite, and rumor was displaced by actuality. On the strength of this fact, one of the tent-store proprietors hastened to follow up on an idea that festered in his brain. He made a hurried trip to Stockton to purchase a large stock of merchandise, which he shipped to Merced, at that time the end of the established freight service. Only heavily loaded construction cars carried freight out of Merced to the south.

'Friendly' Conductor

It was a problem how the storekeeper would get his merchandise over to Fresno Station. He made arrangements with a "friendly" conductor, who promised to secretly store the merchandise (which was both wet and dry) in a box car along with construction materials. That was going to be fine!

To avoid the moment of embarrassment of explaining the situation to the construction superintendent at Fresno Station concerning the "illicit freight," the two ringleaders agreed to have the goods unloaded before reaching the station.

As the construction train grew nearer its destination, the crew started throwing off the boxes, bundles, and barrels from among the railroad materials. For a half a mile or more, along the sandy ridge of what is now Belmont Avenue northward, the side of the track was strewn with a motley array of smuggled freight.

It was evening when these strange objects were tossed to the sand. The only living things to observe or create danger to the tossed cargo were the antelope, jackrabbits, squirrels, rattlesnakes, horned toads, lizards, billy owls, and coyotes.

Took Two Days

It took the scheming owner two days to pick up and load into a wagon all the scattered parcels of various sizes and shapes, and then unload and arrange in his tent-house place of business on a lot not far from the railroad station.

This was the "ingenious" way in which James E. Faber opened the first store in the site of Fresno City, making him, according to Winchell, the first merchant and resident. Faber was in business in Fresno for over forty years. He married Miss Mary Whitney of Millerton in 1873. He died in 1930 at the age of eighty-six.

People of the valley could scarcely grasp the speed of expansion in the Fresno area. It had gone from literally nothing—a forlorn, dusty, uninviting spot—to a place of railroad activity in such a short time.

It had been "solemnly asseverated" in *The Golden West*, a book on California, that "in a part of the southern counties, where cattle were so numerous that they swarmed about the telegraph poles to scratch themselves" there had been very little butter, milk, or cheese for human consumption in a journey of two hundred miles. Fresno was one of the "cow counties" in that early day. Sheep-raising was also an important line at that time.

A Million Sheep

Frank Dusy was one of the expansive sheep men. Fifteen years after the establishment of Fresno as a county seat, there was an estimated one million head of sheep in the county, grazing in the mountain range.

Dusy bedded his flocks on a sandy ridge of the courthouse site when he brought them to the station area. About the same time, Jeff James, a large cattleman, was shipping beef cattle to his San Francisco stockyards, when in previous years they had been driven there.

Reflecting on the year of 1872, Winchell grew almost poetic as he wrote:

> It was springtime; the verdant plain was laid with a rich carpet of many hued wild flowers; in the midst were gangs of busy workmen carpenters preparing materials for a depot; trackmen laying ties and rails for the station switches; others building a turntable for the locomotives; the drove of bawling, milling, long-horned cattle — wild as deer — the shouts of the vaqueros urging the animals to the corrals; the bleating sheep; the click of shears as the workers clipped the wool, and the rumble and clatter of the long train as it approached the site.

'Dash for Liberty'

Suddenly a wild steer from the herd breaks away; with his head high, he dashes for liberty. In front of the frantic animal was a strange creature; with a plunging blow from his long, curving horns he struck the tent ropes, ripping every cord from its pegs; down came the canvas on top of goods and proprietor.

That menace to his liberty out of his way, he spied the gangs of workmen who were enjoying the play; but as he dashed towards them, with a bellow of defiance, there was no further inclination to remain as spectators. In the role of leading actors, every man dropped his tools and did his best to beat the race for the shelter of the cars; and just as the victor had routed all his foes, the whirling nooses of two reatas fell around his great horns and he was promptly rushed back to his herd. Fresno, 1872!

We have noted something of the gold that created the economy and developments of Fresno County; the stockmen and their activities and experiences; the planting of great grain fields; the coming of the all-important railroad and the more important ditches and canals that brought water to the residents, which in turn gave the county its direction toward the top of agricultural leadership. Added to those heralding pointers for the building of an empire were other factors, each to help bring the country to its place in the sun.

Smattering of Mining

There was a smattering of copper mining throughout several sections of the county. There were the timber forests in the mountains, and the logging camps. These brought settlers and money. There had been oil and there had been some cotton experiments.

Slowly creeping into the county were the colony foundations, which were to eventually add greatly to the making of a greater Fresno and the final outcome of the day when it would be a valley metropolis.

In all those things that imparted something to Fresno's great future, there had to have been faith and visions.

As we look at the stupendous growth of Fresno County, we know that here people "dared to dream."

Even so, Leland Stanford and his partners must have dreamed in the room above a hardware store in Sacramento when they planned the railroad into the San Joaquin Valley. As he stood by a gleaming rail track in 1872 in the barren sands of Fresno, perhaps he had a vision of an expanding city under tall trees, interspersed with wide green lawns, vast orchards, industry, business blocks and a great many people.

Well, "nothing happens unless first a dream."

Chapter 17:
The City on the Plains

The merchant Otto Froelich had been the first to leave Millerton, going in April 1872 to Fresno where he bought twenty acres adjacent to the surveyed townsite. He developed his land, building a large two-story house and planting a variety of fruit trees, along with ornamental shrubs and trees. This site was between Van Ness and Park Streets, abutting Divisadero.

Nearly the last to leave the old county seat was Charley Garland, who had been village barber, saloonkeeper, and postmaster. He "trailed at the last fag end of the straggling procession" from Millerton and promptly set up a saloon on Mariposa Street in Fresno, near I Street.

Historians record that by June of election year, 1874, the little town on the plains was going along well. Every lot in the six blocks fronting Mariposa Street had been sold by the railroad company, and many others in adjoining sites.

In August, the new town had four mercantile stores, two fruit stores, two drug stores, three hotels, two law offices, two physicians, one tinsmith, one saddler, two butcher shops, three blacksmiths, one wheelwright, one tailor, one newspaper, one store, three carpenter shops, nine barrooms, a company of painted ladies, railroad buildings and Chinese houses.

A Hundred Buildings

L. A. Winchell adds to the record of the city's expansion that there were a hundred buildings, sixty of them being residences. A photographer came that fall. The town gained its first streetlights when Russell Fleming installed two streetlights in front of his stables, and Bill Lawrenson put two more in front of his saloon.

The first milk delivery was started that summer by A. W. Baker. The patrons set out their pitchers, tin cups, pans, or some other kind of utensil on the fence posts or some other convenience, into which milk was poured (uncovered!), and if the wind did not deposit sand, nor a cat or dog find it first, the customers received their milk, according to the newspaper.

The Fourth of July that year was celebrated with a procession on the downtown streets, led by Justice Thomas Pryce. The editor of the paper read the Declaration of Independence. The freight depot was gayly decorated, and people assembled there. Judge E. E. Winchell gave the day's oration.

In the fall, Otto Froelich and Charles H. Barth opened the first banking business, which they carried on in rented quarters.

The wealth of the county had, in six years, increased from eight hundred thousand to approximately seven million dollars.

'Drunks Plentiful'

The newspaper recorded: "The town grew rapidly . . . hotels are crowded . . . whisky flows rapidly and steadily . . . drunks are plentiful . . . six fights and knockouts in one day, a dull day at that!" It also protested about the presence of "the parasites that feed on a prosperous community." Editor J.W. Ferguson continued by writing, "Thieves and bummers are plenty; they should be ordered to 'vamoose the rancho' or better yet, the contents of a few six-shooters will get rid of the nuisance."

The streets and the alleys in the town," wrote the early historian Paul Vandor, "were in a disgustingly filthy condition." It seems the vacant lots were in the same condition. "They were covered with old bones, hats, boots, dead dogs, decaying vegetable matter, old tin cans and the like, and in consequence is a most disgusting and pestilence breeding effluvia constantly pervading the atmosphere."

Brick buildings were being talked about. On September 9, according to Vandor, "The first brick building in town is announced to be the one that Dixon and Faymonville will erect on the north side of Mariposa between H and I." Froelich and Barth "will erect another for their bank immediately east, and C. G. Sayle talked also of erecting a brick structure."

Election Successful

The school building tax election was a success with fifty votes cast for it, two against it, and plans were made for a school building to cost about $3,000 or $4,000. The school term opened in September that year in an upstairs room of the Booker Building at Tulare and H streets.

A citizens' meeting was held in late September to plan for a clean-up program before the day of the laying of the cornerstone for the projected new courthouse that was held on October 8.

Acclaimed was "the dawning of a new era in the history of the town of Fresno."

Temporary arrangements had been made for the use of the county officials.

During the last week of September, a stream of teams hauling wool, grain, wood, and lumber rolled into town, giving it a busy, brisk appearance. Seventeen teams were counted at one time down on H Street, thirteen of them with four or six teams pulling. It was a bustling village.

Forty Teams a Day

Immigrants were coming to the area in wagons as well as on the trains. As many as forty teams a day drove in. Many of the families were heading for the Kings River country.

The year included some conflict with the Chinese who sought to settle in the town. This did not "set well" with the White residents and the town agent decided to sell no more lots to Chinese. The Chinese were establishing businesses, but a pledge-signing campaign was planned to canvass the people for keeping them out, establishing racial segregation in Fresno. The excluded Chinese settlers retreated "across the tracks," establishing Chinatown.

Before the year ended, the Millerton post office was changed to Fort Miller, with Charles A. Hart as postmaster. This act, said historian Vandor, "expunged even the last official record of the existence of the pioneer county seat."

In October, the cornerstone laying for the future courthouse in Fresno was held. During that same month, the supervisors met in session in the hall above a liquor establishment on Front (H) Street. The temporary building that had been erected for the county business was not large enough to hold the board and its contingents. The use of this upper room was donated by the owner for the sum of one dollar for as long as needed.

Cold and Fog

1874 had been eventful. As it came to a close, there was a spell of unprecedented cold and fog. There had been no rain for a month.

In town, Christmas passed quietly. "Of course," said the official news organ, "the usual amount of eggnog had been drunk and a few drunken fights occurred."

There were several hundred people in the town now. The little plains pioneer town had about all any such town could ask for. Looking back, its happy accident of birth was well worthwhile.

The lodestar had its direction.

"What is the city but its people?" Shakespeare said. Fresno's answer was in wearing its crown well.

Chapter 18:
The Courthouse Site

The first site selected for the county courthouse at Fresno was not the location on which it was eventually built. The railroad company made a generous donation of four blocks for county grounds, which were lettered on the recorded may as A, B, C and D. The lettered squares are bisected by Fresno Street—east and west—and by O Street—north and south. The location was on higher ground, with a more commanding view than the site upon which the building was eventually erected.

When the county officials at Millerton discovered the location that the railroad company had selected for them, they "hit the ceiling," in modern parlance. The original plan by the company was to make Fresno Street the town's main avenue, the widest of any, and it would run from a planned fine railroad building to the courthouse square.

The established center of the town at that point was on H Street, across from the depot.

Officials Appalled

The officials were appalled at the distance from "downtown," and the great size of the donated area.

Such a great extent of desert! Appalling, the idea.

"What will we ever do with it?" It was entirely too much land. They would never be able to walk the distance. All they wanted was a couple of lots. It was too far to walk "over the red-hot plains, without shade, through the tangles of sticky mint, tarweed and tumbleweeds; and thread through the thickets of sagebrush and lupine that covered the site — and no wayside refreshment. Unthinkable!"

L. A. Winchell records their feelings further: "They were in despair at the awful prospect; because after Garland's frontier supply station on Mariposa, near I Street, was left behind, there was no further relief from the ordeals of the arid journey."

Fresno Street had originally been planned by the Central and Finance Company (a subsidiary of the Central Pacific Railroad) as the only eighty-foot-wide business thoroughfare in the city.

Main Street

It would be the main arterial street in the town, although at that time it was obstructed in the center by a ditch (partially covered) from M. J. Church's flour mill at N and Fresno Streets. The ditch carried the surplus water, supplied by Fancher Creek, out to the sparse plains.

This original site was platted for the city and filed with the Fresno County recorder in Millerton on December 12, 1873, shows the courthouse to face Fresno Street. The lots were bounded by Merced, Mariposa, N and P streets.

Most of the privately owned businesses and improvements were grouped on H Street, facing the projected depot, or creeping over onto Mariposa Street.

Read this from the Winchell history:

They sent envoys with a tearful memorial to the railroad magnates. 'Have mercy! Give us something near 'town.' Swap lots with us, or we are ruined! Upon consideration of those pleadings, the railroad officials did swap lots with them and granted the supplicants grounds close enough to the harbor to enable them to reach the courthouse without too great mental and physical disturbance; yet, though the prospect was less depressing, they still looked the gift horse in the mouth. "Grounds! What the immortal Jehosaphat do they expect us to do with all that ground? Hold a rodeo on it?

And so, the courthouse park is where it is, instead of on the more commanding site wisely chosen by the donors.

Deed to Property

A deed to the exchanged property, Blocks 93, 94, 105, and 106, was made on April 29, 1874 "to be used for the erection of a courthouse thereon and for other county purposes."

The building that was to be erected for temporary use contained only four rooms. It was a rough boarded structure. The officers and their county archives moved over to the new location on September 25, 1874.

They adjusted themselves as conveniently as possible in the new quarters. The clerk and recorder occupied one room. Another was given to the sheriff and the tax collector.

The district attorney had his office in the anteroom of Farrar's Magnolia Saloon on Front Street. The assessor had similar quarters. They were all about as scattered about town as they had been in old Millerton before the first county courthouse had been built.

Locations Purchased

When it seemed certain that there would be a courthouse, the location decided upon, the date set for removal, and the residents of Millerton had seen the handwriting on the wall, desirable locations in Fresno City were investigated and purchased.

When the shift started, future townsmen of Fresno bought lots near Front Street near the business section, or on higher grounds, near the courthouse square, or on suburban sites.

A. Y. Easterby and Moses Church had given assurance that water would be conveyed to the new townsite. Upon the water problem hung the future of the town and community. The railroad founders staked their all on water to make the town so that it could be the produce shipping point of the great interior valley.

Plan-Making

Now that the county officials were more or less resigned to their future business and county location, things settled down according to plan, making space for the courthouse and for the town.

The newspaper continued its career in counting the drunks and publishing real estate sales and the names of newcomers. Without its gossip, there might have been dull days in that library-less town with no schools, churches, or recreation other than the saloons.

Those things would come. In the meanwhile, people got busy constructing the courthouse.

Laying the Cornerstone

October 8, 1874 was a red-letter day for the folks in the new town of Fresno. The town had had the equivalent of a face-lift. The streets and alleys were as clean as the Citizens' Clean-up Committee could get them. All the residents, young and old, and the transients (who had come to work on the construction of the new courthouse) were decked out in their best bib 'n' tucker and were out in the fine October air.

It was the long-looked-for day of the laying of the cornerstone for that new courthouse that would soon rise on the sandy plains of soil near downtown Fresno.

It was quite a different day than the one when the first county courthouse had been presented to the town of Millerton back in 1867. The first county courthouse, though long waited for and badly needed, came into use "unhonored and unsung."

Day of Rejoicing

Not that way in bustling, brisk-moving Fresno. The latest courthouse plan was feted from the busy early hours of the day when plans were being carried out to make it a day of rejoicing, fun and pleasure, and no hopes deferred.

The day was pleasant, and the heavens were overcast with just enough clouds to prevent the glaring sun from pouring over the assembled people. A light rain fell at noon, purifying the air and making the day refreshing.

The ladies and children were there. It was an occasion to dress up for. The men must have strutted some, for it was a big day indeed, especially for those who would have a part in the ceremonies. Equally as important for the ones who would be working inside the walls of the courthouse-to-be, when that fine building would rise from the sands. It was so for all the settlers, no matter where they worked or what they did.

It would be a help to the numberless small farmers in the eighteen-year-old county, for the grain ranchers, the men of the logging camps in the mountains and the cattlemen in the foothills. It was a great day for the valley.

Opening Rites

The opening rites were set for one o'clock, just after the usual dinner hour, which in that era was at midday. Perhaps on that important day with everyone wanting to be downtown, the dinner would be a sandwich, or at the most, lunch, with the hope of dining in the evening in one of the downtown restaurants.

The affair was under the Supervision of the Masonic Lodge, which was mostly composed of the brothers from Merced. Most Worshipful Grand Master Isaac S. Titus was on hand to dedicate the future courthouse.

The Independent Order of Odd Fellows participated with the county officials and citizens. There were many visitors from Stockton, Merced, Lathrop, Visalia, and other areas of the valley.

The procession that marched down Mariposa Street was led by Woodman's brass band from Stockton. They marched to the site of the courthouse to be where the ladies were seated on the platform.

A choir opened the ceremonies with singing. The choir was composed of Mmes. J. C. Hoxie, William Lambert, William Faymonville, A, W. Burrell and S. W. Geis, with Mrs. Emily Phillips at the organ. History does not inform us what songs were sung.

The Address

District Attorney C. G. Sayle, on behalf of the county supervisors, addressed the assembly. The address is quoted below:

> Ladies and gentlemen — the Honorable Board of County Supervisors on behalf of the citizens of Fresno County are now about to commence the erection of the grandest and noblest edifice that has ever been planned in this valley.
>
> The said edifice when completed is expected to stand the storms of winter and the heat of summer, for the period of 1,000 years, or more and in order to perpetuate the present history of this county, the Board of Supervisors deem it their duty, in accordance with ancient customs, to invite the Most Worshipful Grand Master of Free and Accepted Masons of the State of California, to lay the cornerstone of said edifice, that they may deposit the usual and items of history for the benefit of future generations, when by the lapse of time this edifice shall have crumbled to dust.

In Cornerstone

After the ritualistic ceremonies were over, the following articles were deposited in the cornerstone at the northeast corner of the building:

Copy of the act of the Legislature, fixing the county seat at Fresno City.
Copy of act authorizing the issuance of courthouse and jail bonds.
Copy of courthouse and jail bond.
Copy of last joint report of the county auditor and treasurer of the county.
Copy of Great Register of county.

Names of county officers.

(The above articles were contributed by the supervisors.)

Copies of Fresno Expositor, May 18, 1870 and October 7. 1874.

San Francisco Examiner, October 5, 1874.

Daily Alta Californian, October 7. 1874.

Sacramento Record, October 7. 1874.

Oakland Daily News, October 6, 1874.

Dixon and Faymonville's map of Fresno County, and map of the town of Fresno.

Holy Bible, contributed by Dr. Lewis Leach. (One historian claims it was the only Bible in town. at least the only available one.)

Business card of Thomas Whitlock and James Young, carpenters.

One $20 gold piece, contributed by A. W. Burrell.

One $10 gold piece; one $5 gold piece; one $2.50 gold piece; one $1 silver coin; one half dollar. one quarter dollar; one ten-cent piece, and one 5-cent, silver coins; one; 3-cent and one 2-centnickel and copper coins of the United States — all contributed by the supervisors.

List of sheriffs of the county (J. Scott Ashman, incumbent making the contribution.)

Historical notes on the first 20 years of the valley, containing a copy of the original Treaty of Peace between the Indigenous peoples and whites, made at old Fort Barbour in 1851; and a copy of the muster roll of the Volunteer Battalion of 1851 under Major James D. Savage, contributed by Dr. Lewis Leach and W. T. Rumble.

Nineteen items went into the cornerstone.

The Oration

After the Masonic rituals were over, Judge E. C. Winchell, at the request of the supervisors, gave the oration that had been prepared by District Judge A. C. Bradford, who was absent.

That evening Magnolia Hall nearly buckled its walls with guests, with 150 couples in attendance. The dance lasted until one-thirty in the morning when the Merced excursion car came for the guests and music. The supervisors had appropriated two hundred dollars for the expenses of the day. After the bell receipts were turned in and the books were balanced for the day and evening, there was a sum of sixty-six dollars left, which was contributed to the school fund. (This was the first stirrings of school interest in the county.)

The county and the city had gone up several notches. The lodestar pointed high for Fresno County and its forwarding child, the little city. They both wore the badge. The ribbons had been cut.

All the vagrant cows that had been taken up under the trespass act could go back to browsing in town. The editor of the *Expositor* would not have to leave out anymore "live ads" to make room for the dedicatory news. The next week there was a circus and World Fair in town.

Chapter 19:
The Turn of the Tide

The Fresnoites of both city and county were jubilant about the new courthouse. They had entered into the thrills and excitement of the day when the cornerstone was laid. The old-timers of the county had waited twelve years for their first courthouse in their historic old town of Millerton. They had known what waiting meant.

What had that sturdy old brick and granite building meant to them? Still standing on the high, sandy shore of the San Joaquin River, it seemed to wear a cloak of brooding bitterness, looking out over the lonely area. Still young in physical accouterments, it was not yet ready to give up the ghost and could still stand up and be counted with the best of them.

As the pioneers looked at it in memory, did they wonder why, as a town and as individuals, they had accepted that first courthouse with apathetic indifference? Why had they not wanted to have a day of excitement and fun, a little fanfare and joy when it had been completed?

The mining town, battered by storm and wind, rain and flood, had needed a courthouse. They received it, but it was as though it were an intangible thing, the way they failed to honor it.

New Field

The election had given them the stimulation of a move to a new field of endeavor. Things looked well for the future. The new courthouse would be a symbol of orderliness, organization, security, and power to lead them onward. It was to be a handsome thing too. Soon all roads would lead to Fresno.

And the Johnny-come-latelies? They were taking all these things for granted, even the courthouse that was steadily reaching completion and had been no worry for them.

Were they a new breed, coming into the valley from here and there, settling in town with business ventures, taking up homestead land, or buying outright if they had the cash? They accepted the railroad, too, and the water, most casually. Perhaps they had a vision to blend with the experiences and visions of the old-timers and together they would produce something fine and grand that would point the way to the great city and county of the days to come.

Together, the old-timers and the newcomers would become a new band of pioneers as they watched the fashioning of the new courthouse, which was really a symbol. They had enjoyed a big town party. One for the record: music, speeches, a parade, dancing.

Springtime

Fifty-eight years later, Historian L. A. Winchell wrote of the springtime of that early Fresno:

Springtime spread its wonderful robes of flowers over the plain, and all around the workers — to the very walls of the courthouse — the ridge blazed with the flame of the royal poppy.

Here at sunrise one morning, curiously drawn toward the red walls of the building, a band of antelope ranged their ranks in cavalry front and stood like statues, inquiring the strange danger, until a moving enemy startled them in column flight to the far, unbroken horizon.

The antelope had met civilization, looked on, and left in a blaze of floral beauty to retire to a more secluded area.

The spring of 1875 passed into summer. By August, the copper dome over the courthouse was crowned with Minerva, who in her plastic civic robes, stood guard over the little new town to remind the citizens of her wisdom in the industries of peace and the arts of war.

Accepted Design

Back in the spring of 1874, proposals had been invited through the press of San Francisco and Sacramento, for building the courthouse. The supervisors accepted the design of A. A. Bennett, state architect. A Sacramento firm, the California Bridge and Building Company, was given the contract. Alfred W. Burrell was president of the firm.

The contract was let for $56,370.

The last act the board of supervisors passed in the old courthouse at Millerton was to authorize a bond issue for $60,000 for building a new courthouse for the county.

With money available, fine plans, and the constant immigration into the county, not to speak of the railroad and the water, how could things go wrong?

Fresno had started from nothing in terms of development by settlers. As 1875 came to an end, the town was still "not much of a town, a handful of houses in a desert of sand." There was more unoccupied space than there was occupied.

Built-up Block

The only solidly built-up block in those first years was the one on the Front Street block, facing the railroad station. That block was afterward turned into a park, under a ninety-nine-year lease to the city, and on which the Chamber of Commerce building was later erected. That building is no longer standing.

The railroad block was, for many years, "an eye-sore, a muddy water hole in winter, a bed of dust, sand and refuse heaps at other times and anything but an inviting front entrance into the city from the railroad," as Paul Vandor described it.

Another newspaper was started in 1875, called the Weekly Review. The publisher was C. A. Heaton, former partner of the *Expositor* editor. The Review lasted only nine months. The *Expositor's* editor, the so-called molder of opinion, stated that "one paper can live in Fresno County while two are sure to starve."

The county register listed 1,640 names.

August saw the completion of the courthouse. It was accepted by the supervisors on August 19, and the board met for the first time in the new building on September 6.

Chapter 20:
The Eventual Year of 1875

Life in Fresno County's seat of government in 1875 sailed along on waves of enthusiasm. The little frontier town, sophisticated and venturesome, conscious of its potential greatness in growth and productive wealth, was still that huddle of "a handful of houses on a desert of sand," according to a resident named R. W. Riggs in 1878.

It lived, breathed, and grew in the full cognizance of the fact that it would be anchored to permanence. Looking back on that long ago time, it seems rather mystical the way it leaped forward in its infancy into history.

In May, Simon Henry, formerly a hotelman, livery-stable-man and blacksmith at Millerton, completed his large hotel, calling it "Henry House." His business was successful, becoming Fresno's leading hotel. Its two-and-a-half stories provided plenty of room for its patrons. A carriage was provided to carry guests to and from the depot. This building was located on Tulare in the block between J and K Streets.

Founder of Party

The now well-known Dr. Chester Rowell, a newcomer in Fresno, who was to become the founder of the local Republican political party and founder of the Fresno Republican newspaper with deep-seated activities in civic and state affairs, built a home on the southeast corner of Tulare and K (Van Ness) Streets.

In August of 1875, a corps of engineers with a large force of workers began the operation of laying out roads and digging holes for the planting of avenue trees for a colony.

The W. B. West nursery company of Stockton contracted to supply trees and vines; an agent was sent to Spain to select the best grape varieties. W. S. Chapman, a prominent landowner in the area, imported thousands of muscatel cuttings to plant in the Fresno area. For this great project, Bernard Marks was the ringleader—his vision and foresight of the county's potential brought about the first colony in an expansive system of such settlement planning.

First Visit

In July, the town had the first visit of a candidate for governor for political reasons. The occasion was a Democratic rally, with William Irwin as the candidate for governor.

Crop failures had greatly checked the growth of the town that summer.

The *Expositor's* editor was moaning through his columns that it was "a disgrace that a town as large as Fresno should be without a church edifice, because a town without a church looks a little uncivilized." At this point, Paul Vandor noted, "Millerton never had one."

The new courthouse building was accepted in August by the supervisors, and in September, the first janitor for the courthouse was appointed.

Excursion Rates

The Central Pacific Railroad was offering excursion rates between San Francisco and Fresno that were good for ten days so that visitors could visit the valley and examine the lands of the Central California Colony.

Martin Theo Kearney was first mentioned in the month of September in connection with his exhibition "of an enormous peanut vine with its roots crowded with nuts in all stages of growth." The plant was grown on irrigated land at the Gould ranch near the town of Fresno. Kearney took the plant to San Francisco to exhibit it at the Mechanic's Fair.

This year, the first oranges in the county were grown at W. Hazelton's ranch on the Kings River. Alfalfa was selling at twenty-two dollars a ton.

The town of Kingsburg received its permanent name that winter, having formerly been called Wheatville.

Social Life Beginning

Social life was opening up for Fresno residents. A daily stage line was running between Fresno and Centerville; Centerville was the most populous town in the county at that time.

Noticeably, there was "a transformation from a desert to a flower garden, and vineyards and orchards from the wild grass plain to the cultivated farm home," historian Vandor recorded.

By the end of 1875, there were fifty-four people living in the new colony outside the city's area, including eighteen children.

A persuasive advertisement went out from the Colony's headquarters. Displayed with the zenith of a printer's art, it set forth:

> Better Than City Property —A Homestead with an Income! Persons of Sedentary or Confining Situations may Establish a Healthful and Delightful Business and Acquire an Elegant and Paying Homestead in Four or Five Years by a Moderate Monthly Payment in the Central Colony of Fresno, and Need Not Retire

from Their Present Business until the New One has Become a Paying Institution! —Twenty Acres of Raisins are Worth $5000 a Year! Twenty Acres of Prunes are Worth $10,000 a Year! A Small Monthly Payment will Secure a Twenty-acres Tract in the Suburb of Fresno, a Rapidly Growing Town—Only Nine Hours from San Francisco by Rail—

The Perfection of California Climate! No Fever and Ague! The Natural Home of the Fig, Citron, Raisin, Prune, Olive, Walnut, Almond, Orange, Lemon!

For pamphlets and particulars apply to "Dixon and Faymonville, Fresno.

So ended four years of Fresno City.

Chapter 21:
The New Courthouse

Now all roads (in the county) would lead to Rome! The event was not a climactic affair. The great phase of the new courthouse progression had come with the laying of the cornerstone. The anti-climax of the building of the courthouse was spread out in the interim. Eleven months had passed since the great event of the cornerstone laying and the time when the new building was ready for use.

It was now September, and the days were probably still warm with the stifling heat of summer. The nights would have been gentle, promising the abatement of the summer climate. But what did it matter? Fresno had indeed reached another milestone on its way to greatness.

For many months, the citizens had not needed to travel long distances by slow vehicles or by horseback to reach the old county seat. There was also no longer the inconvenience of running about town from office to office for various county errands of official nature. The county's business could now be handled within one building.

In His Glory

The *Expositor's* editor must have been in his glory. Here he could dart from room to room, from story to story, for stories and news. Here in this gleaming white building, constructed "to last an endless time," even his broadest visions could not compass what awaited the little town that had started from nothing.

Author Eugene Fitch Ware said, "No town can hope prosperity and trade unless the press shall vigorously aid." The records of Fresno County prove the *Expositor* did its best to bring all that to pass.

The gleaming copper dome was crowned with Minerva by August 1875. On the 19th of August, 1875, the building was delivered to and accepted by the county supervisors, and on the sixth day of September, the board met for the first time in the new quarters. Pioneering experiences were now a thing of the past.

Built of brick with granite trimmings and covered with cement, the building stood sixty by ninety-seven feet, three stories high. Plaster figures of Justice ornamented the front and side window arches. The building was fifty-seven feet above the grade and 112 feet to the top of the cupola figure of Minerva.

The basement was designed for a six-cell jail. Eight hundred thousand bricks went into the construction of the original building.

The designer was A. A. Bennett. a California State architect. An Oakland, California building construction firm secured the contract to build the courthouse and A. W. Burrell, president of the firm, was an active citizen during the time of construction.

Early Years of the Courthouse Park

In the spring of 1876, an ornamental fence was erected around the courthouse, enclosing about five acres. The remainder of the grounds were not utilized by the county but were left free for use for revival meetings and baseball games; they were a common cut-off pathway for shortening distances across town. Schoolboys made ample use of the park land.

Later, the railroad grantors protested the use made of the leftover county grounds and insisted that the grantee of the land conserve its gift according to the terms of deed. In 1883 the park square was fenced in, in regular "ranch fashion" with redwood posts and heavy boards.

Between 1878 and 1888, land around the courthouse was landscaped as a park and was improved through the years by planting.

In the early 1880s, Gus Whitthouse, a former deputy sheriff, took on the job of doing some planting around the magnificent building, which cried for trees and shade and bordered walks to beckon people to pause on the wide expanses of the undeveloped land. He planted pines, cedars, and umbrella trees. The pines died and the umbrella trees came down to be replaced by elms and hardwoods.

First Occupants

The first occupants of the new offices as listed in the Winchell history were J.B. Campbell, district judge; Gillum Baley, county judge; J. Scott Ashman, sheriff and tax-collector; C.G. Sayle, district attorney; Major M. B. Lewis, surveyor; T. O. Ellis, Superintendent of schools; A. Thorne, treasurer and H.C. Daulton, Austin Phillips and J. N. Musick, supervisors.

As time went on, the county's business increased space for archives and working quarters were so congested that extensive additions had to be made. Two large wings were added in 1893, and interior changes were made in the older part of the building. This work was completed in December 1893 at a cost of $99,387, with an additional outlay for new furniture.

Fresno County Courthouse was built in Fresno in 1882. This illustration shows how it looked at the turn of the century. (S. Bybyk)

Caught Fire

On the night of July 29, 1895, the enlarged, winged courthouse caught fire up in the copper-sheeted dome. The glare lit up the entire townsite. The flames were so high that the fire apparatus could not reach them. The dome, built two years before, was 223 feet from the ground and it became "a veritable forest of timbers," as a strong north wind added force to the fire. The dome finally collapsed upon the south wing, carrying with it tons of timber. Wreckage was on the third and second floors of the original (central) structure. The loss was over seventy-five thousand dollars.

They made repairs. Business increased as the county's wealth grew, and the little city of the plains kept up with the county's expansion. Population increased; land became more valuable; farms were richer; agricultural crops went to the top in value and quantity.

The agricultural capital was casting shadows. The re-built courthouse was eventually torn down and replaced by a modern courthouse that was completed in 1966.

Chapter 22:

The Lone Republican of Fresno County

Fresno, an offshoot of Mother Mariposa, the County, had come of age. It was officially, as far as the records stood in Sacramento, still "Frezno" County. The name has probably never been changed! Did it matter? Fresno was "going places" anyway, as soon as it got its legal independence as a county.

In 1856, the apron strings were cut. The county stood at the threshold of its new entity, on tiptoe and chomping at the bit to be on its own. It threw itself into the maelstrom of organizational activities and the political situations of the day.

From its birthdate of its status as a county, it began to forge ahead. In 1850, the entire area of Mariposa County had 4,879 residents. Four years after it became a county, Fresno County had 4705, nearly as many as Mariposa.

Property Value

In 1856, the county had a property value of $431,403.60 and paid taxes to the tune of $7,345.96. It had all the basic industries. It was still a mining county, and its lumber industries were well established. Agriculture was well on its way to prosperity. The military installation just next door to the county seat was an attraction for newcomers.

The long trip to the city of Mariposa had become quite an expensive situation for both the county and individuals.

The petition in 1856 to the State Legislature for countyhood resulted in the enabling statute of April 19. The creative enactment came next on May 26. Millerton, as the most populous settlement in the county, was as a matter of course considered to be the first county seat. The May 26 meeting was held for the purpose of arranging for a June election for county officials and to vote legally on the organization of a county, which was a foregone conclusion.

Fresno's birth year, 1856, was one of consequence in the State. Along with such things as the Vigilance Committee, it was a presidential election year. At the election held in November, Fresno County went:

Buchanan 218

Fillmore 123

Fremont 1

No Secret

Vandor reports in his history of Fresno County: "The identity of this Republican or Whig voter was no secret. He was William Aldridge, and of an age when the younger called him 'Dad.'"

Aldridge was a choresman, according to Paul Vandor, at Payne's trading post in Coarse Gold, about the largest voting precinct in the county. Aldridge also mined in Fine Gold. He took on his title as the "Lone Republican" when Lincoln ran for presidency the first time.

The polling place was in Captain Mace's garden, where Captain Mace was the judge of the election. Voting by ballot had not yet been put into action, and each elector announced orally his choice for the various offices. There could be no secret about the voting.

In Coarse Gold at the 1856 election, there were two Copperheads—a faction of anti-war Democrats—working in the mines. Their last names were Davis and Hill. They were both viewed as undesirable citizens, and they were later suspected of terrorizing and robbing the Chinese.

Davis and Hill made boasts that included slurs about some people not being allowed to vote in the election. Aldridge went to Captain Mace, who arranged quietly for Aldridge to declare his vote, having armed guards standing by.

Hill got into trouble some time afterwards in Indian Gulch in Mariposa County and was killed by a deputy sheriff. Davis disappeared and no one ever knew what became of him.

Quiet Man

Aldridge was a quiet, unassuming man, and had many friends among the Democrats. (They could afford to be generous with a situation like they had politically!) Aldridge's one vote could turn no tides.

One of the candidates for governor had heard of Aldridge and sent him a fine new hat. Aldridge refused to wear the hat until there would be a Republican majority in the county. The poor man never got to wear his fine hat as he died before that day arrived. At least he was respected for his convictions.

Fresno County was a Democratic stronghold in the early years. This came from the fact that there were many Southern people in the county, and it was made stronger by others who came during or after the Civil War, all with similar sympathies.

Lone Herald

Aldridge, standing on his political viewpoint, was the lone herald of another "dyed-in-the-wool" Republican almost two decades later—Dr. Chester Rowell. The latter came in 1874 to the fast-progressing county and named the newspaper he established for his political party— "The Fresno Republican." He was, in fact, the father of the Republican Party in Fresno County. He established the paper in 1876 and through it, he rose to political influence and power.

Dr. Rowell believed in partisan politics and put his faith in his party above all others. He respected the right of others to have their choice of party politics. In 1879, Dr. Rowell was elected to the state Senate, even though the county was still a strong Democratic set-up. He was the first Republican ever elected to the county office.

He was re-elected to the senate several times. He was appointed to the University of California as a regent in 1891 and continued in that capacity until his death in 1912. He was also mayor of the city of Fresno. He held influence over many worthwhile activities as he helped to build the town upward. His interests and appointments and elections are numerous; along with his many responsibilities, he practiced medicine. He was an outstanding citizen and generally loved well by the people of Fresno.

Chapter 23:
A Long Christmas Ago

Christmas. What was it like, in the long ago time when Fresno County was building itself up, slowly but surely, on the sands of time? Speaking of sand, there was plenty "and then some!" on the shores of the San Joaquin River and the Kings River, as well as the great plains that reached far beyond the new county seat.

Christmas today is utter sophistication and modernity compared to the early years of the county. Without implying that there is no sincere inner joy of the Yuletide now, the activities, secular and religious, keep in step with the decades and set new standards, weaving in the legends and traditions of a century ago.

Let's Reminisce

Let us reminisce about the old Yuletide in early Fresno County.

To numerous people of the early mining groups of the 1850s and 1860s, the name Christmas was merely a word, just a date on the calendar; to others, it was a memory, perhaps unspoken. The date of the day had no impact on the activities of those who were adventuring on the sandy Californian shore where they slept in tents or out under the stars.

Finally, however, families came to the river settlement, but there was still little in the way of Christmas celebration.

When Millerton became a community, there were a few homes that hung stockings on bed posts, doorknobs, from a chair back, or any improvised place handy for Santa Claus.

Nothing Formal

No formal activities were planned, but there were the hotel dining rooms where elaborate dinners were prepared for those who need not stay with the tent homes or the campsite. The frontier saloons, too, did their bit for the holiday observance. A dance might be planned and enjoyed by those who yearned for festivities.

The old courthouse at Millerton in its grand days gave a more dignified air to the Yule holidays. People came on horseback, in buggies, buckboards and farm wagons, prepared to linger a few days and get a touch of civilized living to brush away for a time the monotony of their dreary lives.

Many nights they danced the night through, and on until the noon hour, wresting from the occasion a "last desperate bit of joy."

Changed Ways

With the establishment of a county seat, the county people changed some of their ways of living. Rich and dainty items of feminine dress were sent down from Stockton and San Francisco to give grace to the festivities that changed from mere dances to balls. The brand new floors were wonderful for the cheerful feet that stepped off with old-time elegance in quadrilles, Polish dances, the rollicking Virginia reels, and the beautiful old-day waltzes.

When the county seat was moved to Fresno City, a fuller and deeper development of social life was manifested. On December 25, 1875, the populace had its first local entertainment and Christmas tree in Magnolia Hall over the Farrar saloon on Front Street, next to the Einstein store building.

During the early 1880s, Sunday Schools had been organized and appropriate Christmas programs arranged, with presents distributed from the tree. To make it possible that everyone might enjoy each program of the various churches, the activities were all planned for a different night Christmas week.

Christmas Balls

Christmas balls were also held in the new town, and all the hotels and restaurants featured Christmas menus.

In Fresno City's first Christmas holidays, few people set up the traditional trees, for there were few trees to be had at the time. These few were expensive, too, and it was a long trip by team and vehicle to the hills to cut their own.

The fine Christmas ball of 1874 was something to be remembered. The ladies wore silk gowns that "would stand alone," made with voluminous skirts and tight waists, buttoned closely to the form. Earrings dangled, exquisitely wrought of pure soft gold, with large broaches to match.

The men were there in their dignity—with goatees and beards and flowing mustaches, clipped and curly. After the dance, they went merrily down the footpaths to a midnight supper at the French hotel.

Danced Again

After supper, they danced again while rain fell outside. The proper girls had to be home by two or three o'clock in the morning; they braved the low spots of the town that had turned into muddy ponds. The fortunate ones who had come in buggies fared better in the inclement weather.

So Christmas was a gala day after all in old Fresno. It progressed along the years, changing its mode of embellishment and observance, but never changing in the deep spiritual meaning of the day and tradition.

Fresno's Christmas Tree Lane

One of the lovely traditions of Fresno is the annual Christmas Tree Lane. The first lighting of the lane was only a single tree. In 1920, it was lit by Mrs. W. P. Winning, a resident of Fresno, in memory of a lost little son. The lights shining from that one beautiful cedar deodar were very impressive. Like Shakespeare's little candle, how far that string of Christmas lights threw its beams!

Mrs. Winning lit her tree each year, and its beauty grew upon the neighborhood and those who passed along the way. Eventually, someone suggested to the Fig Garden Woman's Club that it would be a nice gesture if others along the boulevard would light their trees.

The lovely line of deodars along Van Ness Boulevard reaches out from tall heights with broad branches and seems to take on the atmosphere of a subdued and shady lane. The Indigenous people say the cedar deodar is "the Timber of the Gods." It is an apt description of the great branching "living Christmas tree."

Acting upon the suggestion of getting others interested in lighting trees, the Woman's Club appointed a committee that set out to further the lighting of the trees, which grew to more than a dozen in the early 1920s. Later, when the Fig Garden Men's Club was organized, it took over the matter of arranging for the continuous business affairs of the lighting of the lane.

Dr. W. W. Leslie was one of the many pioneers in the Christmas Lane perpetuation. In 1927 Dr. Leslie attended the Rose Bowl game and Rose Tournament in Pasadena and was so impressed with the lighted Altadena Lane that he made it a point to discuss with the officials the operating affairs of the southern lane. He shared his knowledge with Fresno's Lane committee, and they raised several hundred dollars to help defray the expenses of the first really big lighted lane.

The list of pioneer workers is too long to list here, but millions of people who have enjoyed the lane through the years are grateful to them. There have now been many decades of yuletide beauty and light from the magnificent old trees of the avenue as the tradition continues.

Chapter 24:
County Post Office in 1879

The January 1, 1879 issue of the *Fresno Weekly Expositor* listed the towns of Fresno County that had official post offices. There were seventeen up to that date. They were Berenda, Buchanan, Borden, Big Dry Creek, Fresno, Fresno Flats, Firebaugh, Huron, King's River, Kingsburg, Kingston, Liberty, Madera, New Idria, Panoche, Toll House and Wildflower.

There were a number of communities that were established and later had post offices, but they had decreased in importance, size, or serviceability and lost their government ratings. Millerton is noticeably missing from the list, due to the removal of the county seat to Fresno. Sycamore also was among the missing, as it lost its hoped-for status as the main railroad town of the valley.

Berenda was a station on the San Joaquin Valley Railroad that contained a store and hotel kept by John Brown. It was the terminus for mail for Buchanan and Fresno Flats in the mountains. It was situated where it is today, in Madera County, then a part of Fresno County. A stage carried the mail to the mountains.

Active Community

Borden, still in existence and located in the same area on the rail line as now, was an active community when Fresno was a barren plain.

It was settled in 1868 and earned its post office status in 1873. It became a trading point for the southerners that made up the Alabama Colony. Borden aspired to the candidacy of county-seat but withdrew before the 1874 election. When it failed as a colony, it was soon practically abandoned, being too near Madera to carry on in the face of the latter's active status.

Buchanan, situated in the foothills in the northern part of the county, had its heyday as a flourishing camp with the discovery of copper veins. A considerable amount of money was expended to make the mines pay, but labor and transportation costs were too high to keep the operations going.

Fresno Flats lay in the mountains near the head of the Fresno River in a mining, farming, lumbering and stock-raising country. The discovery of quartz lodes gave it a flare of glory in 1879. It was only eight miles from the head of the great Madera lumber flume.

Started as a Ferry

Firebaugh started as a ferry on the San Joaquin River. It was situated on good farming land but seems to have been directed to stock-raising. The village was dependent on the Miller & Lux cattle ranch land along the river, and the later grain and alfalfa and stock farms. It was one of the oldest sheep-shearing stations in the county.

Big Dry Creek had a post office in 1870 due to the surrounding prosperous farming community. This was once a dry-farming country, and little effort was made to take irrigation to the lands. It included, besides itself, the settlements of Academy and Mississippi. The region, both socially and industrially, was prominent. Fine granite was found above the Academy region.

Huron, the terminus of the Southern Pacific Railroad branch running west from Goshen, was located in a desolate waste and made little progress in those early years. There was some cereal farming during wet years, and some grazing was carried on.

Official Title

King's River had the official post office title for all the Upper King's River country, including Centerville, one of the main settlements in the county (formerly called Scottsburg) in 1879. Centerville came out in third place for the county-seat in the election.

Kingsburg, on the rail line, was named for the King's River, although it bore the name of Wheatville prior to that. Founded in 1873, it had a brisk grain trade, and later went in for fruit.

Kingston, located near the present-day site of Laton, was once the most prosperous community in the county. The coming of the railroad through the valley decreased its importance.

Liberty Settlement was located on the King's River and the Cole's Slough, and was a forerunner of present-day Riverdale, changing its name in 1875.

Outcome of Enterprise

Madera was the outcome of a great lumber flume enterprise. It was laid out in 1876 by the California Lumber Company on the south side of the Fresno River. It brought lumber down from the pineries some sixty-three miles distant in the mountains to the mill at Madera in the flume.

In 1878, the firm came under the business head of Madera Flume and Trading Company. Madera became the county seat of the county by the same name when it divorced itself from its mother county in 1893.

New Idria, born from the activities of quicksilver mining, eventually became a part of San Benito County by annexation. The inhabitants were mostly Cornish and Mexican miners, the latter numbering 500 when the furnaces were in full operation. The mine was idle for a long time because of costly litigation.

Panoche was a settlement in the valley of the same name in the Diablo mountain range. Stock-raising and farming were the main pursuits.

Toll House, picturesquely located at the foot of the first mountain of the Sierra base, was a bustling lumber depot and shipping point for the mills on Pine Ridge. Settlers in the hills and fertile valleys engaged in the usual farming and stock activities.

Thrifty and Prosperous

Wildflower was the post office name for the Duke Settlement on the Emigrant Ditch, twelve miles south of Fresno. The pioneers were southerners who were thrifty and prosperous.

The land was excellent for farming, and there was an abundance of water for irrigation, furnished by a ditch that was built and owned by the settlers. Cattle-raising was also a pursuit. Vineyards, orchards, truck gardens, hay, and grain were the main items of the Wildflower agricultural pursuits.

Fresno, climbing to the status of a county seat, earned its post office earlier as a railroad station. In 1879, the county was heralded as "a new and wonderful country," though the town was really little more than a village. Downtown blocks had been leveled and trees had been planted. The greatest problem was drinking water. Cows still traversed the vacant lots and footpaths. Four to six blocks in any direction took one to the country, past the last habitation.

But it was to bypass every other community in the valley, regardless of the modest picture of the time.

Chapter 25:
First Schoolhouse

Nearly everyone remembers our very first day of school. Any way you look at it, it's an important event.

At the turn of the twentieth century, you can imagine the children of Fresno County: barefoot boys and girls wearing sunbonnets. They often looked forward to school, attending high school and the schools of their parents' choice—often boarding schools for finishing the young ladies and colleges and universities for the young men and the forward-looking maidens.

Just like the county offices in Fresno's first years when it was nick and tuck to find headquarters for the offices (in both first and second county seats) until the courthouses were constructed, so the same situation arose in schools in the city of Fresno.

Notes Article

I came across an old article that pertains to a beloved school building in Fresno's earlier years. It was written in September 1925 by Ernestine Winchell, a columnist for the Fresno Republican. I think many of you might like to read the first paragraph, especially if it were your beloved alma mater of grammar school days:

Turned around, shoved over, lifted up; superseded, superfluously named and renamed the old white schoolhouse preserves its dignity and its individuality with the patient calm peculiar to all survivors of many useful years. For 45 Septembers its doors have opened to Fresno children: three generations have trod its halls and society and trades, the army and navy and the professions have all been recruited from its student ranks.

Fresno's first school served the children of the city for four years. It was located on Tulare Street, east of the courthouse, and the number of students outgrew the space. The overflow was taught in the Methodist church across the courthouse square.

A New Site

In 1878 the school trustees sold that piece of property and purchased another site from the railroad company, described as block C and bounded by Fresno, Merced, and O Streets. There, on slightly elevated land, which was part of the first donation to the county for court buildings, a schoolhouse was constructed.

The school was a seven-room, two-story edifice. It was a frame building, designed in a dignified style of architecture. It was painted white, and it stood, stalwart and inviting in the glistening valley sunshine. It had a tower with a broad band of gold around it.

The building was constructed of the best materials available for the times. It cost the county $7,000. An additional $3,000 was spent on furnishings and equipment.

The white schoolhouse opened its doors on the first Monday in September of 1879, with a little more than a hundred pupils reporting.

The first roll that year included many nostalgic names of the long-ago era.

The Faculty

Three teachers took care of the three Rs that year. Thomas J. Kirk was the teacher-principal. He taught until 1894 when he became county superintendent of schools and later went to a state office.

Mrs. Euphemia Wren Bramlet was in charge of the intermediate classes. Mrs. Bramlet was a trained educator. Dora Reiss had the youngest children. Miss Reiss later married Ren Faymonville, a relative of Fresno's first mayor, William Faymonville. under the trustee-chairman system.

Miss Reiss' bridegroom built her a nice home at the corner of I and Stanislaus Streets. It was the first brick residence in town. It later, under new ownership, became the show place of the town with ornamental railings on a second story, and with cast-iron statuary in the wide and beautiful grounds.

Building Moved

To make room for the large brick school building that was built in 1902, the little white frame building was moved to the Merced Side of the block and received an additional story. At that time formal names were being applied to the school buildings. The new brick was called Washington Grammar.

The little white schoolhouse was christened Hawthorne, though it was sometimes spoken of as the Central School.

In 1913, a new Washington Grammar School was constructed on Glenn Street, and the older brick building was given the name of Hawthorne. The little old white schoolhouse on Merced was then called Luther Burbank.

Regardless of the changing names, there were many people throughout the years that carried the memory of the little white school building in their hearts.

For a time, the little white building served as a church hall until different buildings were constructed for the denominations that used it.

It had a useful life, that little building that at last had to go with the progress of time.

Chapter 26:
The County Seats Incorporates

According to L. A. Winchell, Fresno County historian of the 1930s, the first attempt to incorporate the City of Fresno was made in June 1874. Fresno City was barely two years of age at that time. The attempt failed, lacking general support. Two years later, the historian recorded that a citizens' committee was appointed to work toward incorporation. This effort was also unsuccessful.

Paul Vandor, an earlier historian of the county, recorded in 1919 that "at a conference in the office of E. C. Winchell, Friday evening, March 22, 1878 .... the subject of the incorporation of the city was made for the first time."

By order of the Board of Supervisors, an election was held on December 1, 1883 in the interests of incorporation, and again the cause was defeated. A special election was held on May 3, 1884 and also met defeat.

Finally Won

Finally, at an election held on September 29, 1885, the city won its fight for its own government. Thirteen years after Leland Stanford ordained his railroad town as Fresno Station, the town had reached this stage of maturity.

The abiding faith of the pioneers, which had become deep-seated with the introduction of irrigation, persisted to another milestone of growth.

In the 1885 election, there were 477 votes cast, 277 for incorporation.

During the incorporation year, the Fresno Board of Trade was organized. It became very active and worked energetically toward Fresno's future. While a booming real estate excitement was raging the Board was neglected by its most prominent and lucrative members. Before officials took measures to abolish the Board, the Fresno Real Estate Exchange came into the picture and effected a reorganization of the Board of Trade. Eventually, the board merged with the Chamber of Commerce.

Elected as city trustees were W. L. Graves, T. E. Hughes, J. M. Braly, A. Tombs, and William Faymonville.

Appointive Officers

Vandor lists the appointive officers of the new regime: clerk and assessor, W. B. Dennett; marshal, C. T. Smith, (who resigned the next year); treasurer, W. H. McKenzie; recorder, S. H. Hill; attorney, H. S. Dixon; and engineer, J. S. Eastwood. Health Board appointees were Drs. A. J. Pedlar, C. D. Latimer, Louis Einstein, W. T. Riggs, and engineer Eastwood. The Health Board was organized in January 1886.

At the time of the election, the school trustees chosen were J. F. Wharton, W. W. Phillips, Dr. C. D. Latimer, G. E. Church, and M. K. Harris.

At the first council meeting held on October 27, John Hurley and Martin McNally were appointed Fresno's first policemen at sixty dollars a month. The marshal was awarded a salary of eighty dollars per month.

The first week the city trustees held nightly meetings until the municipality got started toward good running form. The November 28 meeting saw the completion of 510 sections concerned with city affairs.

Advertising Campaign

When the Board of Trade was organized, an advertising campaign was set in full force. The city was now, as Winchell stated, "conscious of its new plumage, and invited the world to recognize its importance in the lists of civic claims."

The trustees put their collective minds to the many tasks at hand and gave attention to the pressing needs of the little city. For a time, they worked under the handicap of inadequate resources.

Before the year was out, streets were being graded and the numbering of blocks and buildings was ordered.

A volunteer fire company was already housed in a small frame building on the east side of J (Fulton) Street, between Fresno and Merced Streets. The city assumed control of the property in February 1886.

In September, the city purchased its first fire engine, a Silsby, for $2,750, on credit.

In another year, the city fire department had its new two-story brick building, complete with an engine house, city offices, council chamber and firemen's dormitory.

The volunteer fire brigade turned over its engine, hose cart, and hook-and-ladder truck to the city.

Gas and Light Service

Gas and light service was inaugurated in the city in June 1886. In a year, four tall masts bearing incandescent lamps were erected on the courthouse grounds.

In May 1887, the Bank of Central California opened on Mariposa Street with Louis Einstein as president.

The year 1887 was to prove probably the most active of Fresno's early years.

The year of incorporation boasted 3,500 people, according to Winchell. His earlier colleague, Vandor, was more generous with an estimate of 4,000. Incorporation did a lot for the plains city. The newspapers kept the flame alive through the years. Not the least of the reasons why it should incorporate was that there "was a large and unwieldy population that the general administration seems unable to reach." There was, it was pointed out, no power to abate nuisances, to repair streets, to safeguard against fires, or to consistently preserve the peace. The first years of Fresno City are recorded as "free and loose days."

Fresno hoped to be able to say that "her ways are ways of pleasantness, and all her paths are peace."

Chapter 27:
Land Bloom

The little plains city of Fresno that started out with a brand-new railroad in its lap, soon had a brand-new courthouse, and now was itself a brand-new little city, complete with the crown of incorporation. It was setting up its different official departments and divisions. It began to plan for utilities, and in two years Fresno had its first telephone system. The fire department was also set up.

Not Overnight

By 1887, the boom hit Fresno. Not only the city of Fresno, but the county. Advertising became an essential aid to the growth of the city and county.

However, the boom did not burst forth overnight. It had come normally, gradually, a thing of consequence in an eager, avid county.

The county had had many experiences to start it forth on a full-fledged boom. It had found growth by expansion and casting off old things no longer useful, such as a county seat and a courthouse. It had gone through a financial panic. It had returned to normalcy. And it never lost sight of its great natural resources.

From its past experiences, Fresno was to become the Raisin Center, not only of the county, valley, and state, but of the world. By 1887, the area was ready for great expansion. They were receiving new populations to join the settlers who were already established living there. They mostly came from the Middle West, these new agriculturalists entrepreneurs, handmen and craftsmen, to add to the exploits and activities of the progressives of the city and county.

Not Only County

People came not only to the county, but other parts of the valley. The influx of people was also hitting the state—San Diego, Bakersfield, San Jose, Stockton, Los Angeles and the San Francisco Bay cities of Oakland, Alameda, and Berkeley.

Land speculations resulted in finer buildings for businesses and dwellings. Additions were added to the townsite. Farm and suburban lands were divided and parceled out into town lots and annexed to the city. Town lots brought more cash than a vineyard or orchard.

Historian L. A. Winchell said, "Land agents induced attention from Los Angeles boomers; San Francisco took notice and sent scouts. The ripples of the rising tide grew stronger; the waves increased to flood height and the storm of speculation broke in full volume. The boom was on! The year 1887 witnessed the birth of 'frenzied finance.'"

On the Uplift

Real estate business was on the uplift. Real estate offices opened in every available space. Mergers were formed. Speculators organized, and brokers were numerous on the streets. Property changed hands often and typically at added values. Vineyards increased in value from two hundred dollars to six hundred dollars an acre. Every property owner near town split up his holdings to sell in smaller plots.

Excursion trains brought crowds to the center of land excitement. Fares were reduced to encourage people to come into the valley. The streets of Fresno took on the look of a metropolis. It was difficult to find hotel rooms. During the summer months people slept on second-story porches. Private homeowners were urged to rent their rooms to tourists.

The saloons also did a "land office business!" Bars were packed and unknown sums of money were lost and won across the gambling tables. Gold was still the coin of the realm for the old miners still in circulation, but other mainstream currencies were also coming into use.

Two Extra Deputies

When the boom reached its zenith, business was so strong that the county recorder was allowed two extra deputies to take care of the recording of official instruments.

The influx of people was so great that new hotels were built. So many people had caught the speculative fever.

On April 4, 1887, one firm sold twenty-six unimproved tracts in the new Washington Colony to a group of Texans. On another day, thirty-five deeds were recorded, representing more than $100,000 in land deals. There were many days like that.

The *Expositor* featured such transactions. The deals were many, lasting many months. The pace of transactions continued into 1888.

Thomas E. Hughes, who has been called the "Father of Fresno," was one of the active participants in these boom days, nurturing it along with M. Theo Kearney, who came to the county without capital. Both Hughes and Kearney forged ahead in these land transactions.

Top Promoter

By the end of 1888, Kearney was a top promoter, and his Fruit Vale Estate was up for sale. He had ambitious personal plans for building a French-type home on his land, copied after a famous chateau in France.

In January 1887, Timothy Paige and T. C. White set out a vast acreage of raisin grapes, which at the time was considered the largest raisin vineyard in the world.

At the crest of the boom, there were twenty-three raisin and dried fruit packing houses in the Fresno County districts; fourteen were located in Fresno, and the remainder at Oleander, Fowler, Selma and Malaga.

Not only was 1889 the great boom year for land movement, but it was a great building year. Six blocks of Mariposa Street had expenditures of one million dollars expended for business, bank and hotel structures. Fresno, Tulare, and I, J, and K Streets were very much improved by substantial and imposing buildings. By 1890, the pioneer look of the town was disappearing.

Panic Followed

Boom years are often followed by years of depression. This was true for Fresno County. Great fortunes were swept away. Not only did the county seat city suffer from the panic, but many farms were passed from the hands of their owners. The whole valley suffered. For the following ten years, there was a slow comeback.

Once a comeback had been made, Fresno was no longer a village, but a town. By 1890, the county census showed 31,158 in population. Fresno had a total of 10,890 citizens.

It is notable that in 1889 an act was passed deleting the word city from the name of the county seat, and the town became officially Fresno.

Fresno emerged from the boom and then the panic with better streets, more substantial business buildings, and many fine homes.

Agricultural pursuits were taking hold. Cooperatives were starting, and a greater county was in the crystal ball.

One of the new organizations to be born was the 100,000 Club, which sought to attract immigrants to the Valley. The club lived but a short while, but its shadow existed in the actual building up to that figure.

Chapter 28:
Sinks of Dry Creek

Big Dry Creek played an important role in the settlement and political rise of Fresno County. There is said to be a point in the Sierra headwaters where a bucket of water, poured out on the ground, would flow in three directions—into the San Joaquin River, into Big Dry Creek, and into the Kings River. Two additional creeks, Dog Creek and Red Banks Creek, brought water down into the valley where the railroad was to push through and a city would be born. These two waterways joined to bring the water to a thirsty plain. Fancher Creek, rising in the highlands, took off towards the south to add to the water that one day would go into Mill Dutch Canal.

Flowing into a sink (a depression in the land) that would become a vital part of a future city of importance, the waters of the creeks spread out over the surface of the area. What the sun did not take up by evaporation sank into the sandy stretches over which a railroad was built—an event which would echo far into the future of the valley.

Virgin Land

When White settlers first traversed the plains of Fresno County, they found land that had not been developed or cultivated in a Western sense. There were no trees in the region between the foothills and the Fresno Slough. The vast area, unshaded in the glaring summer sun and unimpeded from the raging winds of winter, held no promise of any kind of agricultural future for this backyard of the growing coastal area.

Annual plant life dotted the spring landscapes, bloomed and ripened its seeds under the summer heat, dried up through the autumns and scattered everywhere with the elements, leaving the land to winter rains and frost.

Wild horses roamed the great valley, living off the lush grasses during the growing season. The elk and the antelope ranged over the vast plain.

The White men who came to the hill country of the San Joaquin River and the well-watered land of the Kings River area during the 1850s and 1860s brought cattle in great herds that joined the wild animals roaming the basin. They found the blooming and green plants and the alfilaria (a forage weed) that was tasty and thrived.

The Indigenous people who lived in the hills and on the riverbanks used the valley as hunting ground where they shot game as they needed or desired with bows and arrows.

Waters Came Down

After a generous valley rain and the melting snows of warm days, the waters came down into the plains country and spread over the land. Sand ridges marked the plain and turned the gently moving floods about in all directions, seeping into the soil and evaporating due to the sun's heat. By mid-summer, the whole plain was billowing with dust, filled with dun-colored plant life and scorching sand. The grazing animals drifted to the foothills and riverbanks.

In 1872, the irrigation canal that brought water from the Kings River made use of the Fancher Creek bed as far as was practical, then poured Kings water into Big Dry Creek in later years when the mill ditch was no longer in use.

At the time the irrigation canal brought water from the Kings River, the railroad crossed the San Joaquin River. Near where the two streams were destined to cross, the town was laid out that is now Fresno—the metropolis of the great valley.

Those who came to the area for the first time in the dry season could scarcely believe that the united waters of several hill-born streams had for untold years spread out their rainfall tides in the dry land depressions.

Stacked Out

"Fresno Station" was surveyed and staked out in May 1872 as a townsite in the sink of Big Dry Creek. The railroad had not yet reached the sink, and there was no water closer than the San Joaquin River ten miles away. There was no settlement, not even a shack. It was a forlorn-looking spot. Paul Vandor stated in his history of the county, "No one but an optimist would ever be tempted to settle there." He wrote:

> The old-timer relates that there was not a drop of water to be had on the journey from the settlements on the Kings to Millerton — from river to river — and of course none plain-sward towards the new town which was not on a traveled way; that not a human habitation was passed en route; so desolate was the plain that one could journey twenty miles or more in any direction without so much as finding a brush large enough to cut a horse switch; and so level and unobstructed that long in after years on a bright day the courthouse dome could be discerned by the wagon traveler as far as Centerville, fifteen to twenty miles away.

Provided Channel

As it happened, the growth of the irrigation system provided a channel for normal rainfall for a number of years after the town of Fresno was established. For more than a decade, homes were built and gardens were planted where Big Dry Creek had always poured its waters and where the antelope and elk could come to drink.

In the winter of 1884, a year of great rains, more water came down from the hills through Big Dry Creek, Fancher Creek, Dog Creek and Red Banks Creek than the ditches could carry or the rain-soaked soil could absorb.

Houses, barns and sidewalks, gardens, trees, and hedges, could not withstand the waters, and the flood once more regained its former depression. Basements were filled with water. Families were marooned in their homes. Teams and wagons bogged down. The population of the town that had so "unwittingly been placed" in the sinks of Big Dry Creek, was sunk in its own depression of dismay and astonishment.

For many years, the flood problem confronted the people of early Fresno. Canals were built to help in the situation. The channel of Big Dry Creek was deepened.

From the point where Olive and Blackstone Avenue intersected, Big Dry Creek followed its original course. It diagonally traversed the town until it reached Roosevelt Avenue near Mildreda Street. From there, an artificial canal led the Big Dry Creek water and Kings River water under the Southern Pacific tracks and on for several miles, distributing the flow in the ditches as needed.

Over many early years, great rains and floods played havoc with dismayed residents of the town. Nowadays, one who has occasion to be at the Southern Pacific Depot during a hard rain can well be reminded of the situation in the first few decades of the city, as that section of Fresno was once its main downtown and business district.

Chapter 29:
Shelbyville Swindle

Swindles are bound to happen in any major land boom, and Fresno County was no exception. One of the biggest swindles of the late 1880s and early 1890s in the Fresno County land boom was the Shelbyville affair. Shelbyville, a duly platted town, was the core of a swindle that was conceived by a man from the Midwest who passed through the San Joaquin Valley and bought a section of land.

The purchaser, Guy Webber, was a showman who hailed from a theatrical circuit of the central states. The four sections he bought were at that time a desert wasteland, located near a Southern Pacific railroad station called Jameson.

When Webber returned to his show circuit, he started giving away lots of his California acreage by way of lottery tickets, as an added attraction for an audience.

The Shelbyville swindle, spoken of in later years as Phantom Shelbyville, was legitimate; the land belonged to Webber and he could ethically do what he wished with it. What happened to his buyers might well be questioned though. Hundreds of people held deeds to the town lots in the phantom city of Shelbyville, a town that rounded out its entire life on paper.

Cozy Name

Shelbyville—the town with the cozy name. The name itself had nice connotations and evoked pleasant pictures of a shady village with white picket fences, vine-covered porches, flagstone paths, and grape-laden trellises.

One could conjure up arched entrances to arcades where humanity breezed in and out of little shops. Of course, there would be a plaza, which took the place of the old-time village green where band concerts could be held and was a gathering point for conviviality.

In 1890, the year Shelbyville was paper-born and having a heyday by remote control, the county of Fresno was hurdling its peak in land sales: the county was regarded far and wide as a land flowing with milk and honey. It sounded rather wonderful to the patrons of the faraway theatrical circuit.

The townsite was lavishly described. It was located not far from the celebrated Raisin Center of the world. With little knowledge of what they really had, the show-goers took over their lots on a sort of pig-in-a-poke basis, and little dreamed they were getting land in a desert wasteland.

Many Takers

There were many takers, and they were assured that they were getting a fine town lot in the lush San Joaquin Valley in fabulous California.

There were two certain rewards for them; they could either take possession of the property and live on it, or they could sell it for a good price.

Webber's title to the land was good. He had legitimately paid for it. But the highest value placed upon the lots was $4 each. As he sold his lots, Webber received almost as much money from every lottery owner for the cost of the deed, the notary fees, and seals as if they had paid cash for the lots.

Hundreds of these deeds piled up in the Fresno County recorder's office over the years that followed, due to unpaid recording deeds.

There was a town in Indiana named Shelbyville and it might be assumed that the showman had played in it on the circuit. The printed deeds that were recorded in the county recorder's office were endorsed "Dan'l of Shelby," which may have been the name of some theatrical person.

A Gold Mine

The speculator made good—the lottery scheme proved a gold mine for him.

The earliest deeds were made in Webber's name as grantor, but after a time they carried the name of a man whose last name was Hoytt. Later, the grantor's name appeared as W. H. Whetstone.

The Shelbyville deal was not unique. Someone else followed the pattern in another section of California in which the endorser was named "Sam'l of Posen." Historian Vandor records that the Shelbyville townsite was visible from Jameson Station on the Southern Pacific rail line, one-half mile northeast of the depot, between the depot and the San Joaquin River.

Alkali Land

The land about the Shelbyville townsite was purest alkali land, on which, says Vandor:

> ...not even a mortgage or salt grass could be raised, and not unlike the country around the Dead Sea in Palestine, where the birds fly high in passing over it. West and south of Jameson Station, there is good land, within a half mile of the depot, but Shelbyville was in a class of its own. Value it had once as grazing land, but with the bringing of water for irrigation the alkali in the subsoil was forced to the top and not a blade of grass was on the land. The leanest and hungriest coyote or jack-rabbit that crossed the plain to the wheat ranches beyond made a detour rather than shortcut across inhospitable and desert Shelbyville.

By the time Whetstone got into the town lot muddle, the panic of 1902 hit the country. Of the hundreds of non-resident owners of Shelbyville, few had kept up the tax payments. The largest part of the tract was sold for the unpaid taxes. Vandor records that the land was regarded as so worthless that by 1920 the assessor had not listed them for years.

Shelbyville was only one of several land schemes that were put over in those early years of Fresno's past. It was something like O'Henry said of some other affair: "It was beautiful and simple as all truly great swindles are."

Chapter 30:
Pioneer Physician

Dr. Lewis Leach was among the outstanding men who pioneered Fresno County. After he graduated from a medical school in St. Louis, Missouri, he practiced medicine for two years. He became interested in going to California and immediately found himself in the midst of adventure. He organized a party in Salt Lake City, and on their way west they met a party of thirteen families who had become lost.

The two companies joined, and the young doctor was made the leader. They came westward through the southern route. The family groups continued to Los Angeles from the Mojave River; Dr. Leach and his initial party cut through over the mountains to the Kern River country.

They met a party of settlers who had recently survived a conflict with Indigenous people at Woodville, near the present-day site of Visalia. Dr. Leach and his party shared their food supplies with the refugees and helped to bury the dead. It took them twenty-five days to reach the San Joaquin River where they came upon the mining camp and store at Gravelly Ford and had their first real meal in all that time.

All members of the Leach party went to work in the mines except the doctor. He had made up his mind to go back east when he was asked to see a young man who had been wounded in the conflict at Woodville. He had escaped and had reached the river settlement at Millerton to spread the alarm of the uprising. The arrow wounds had caused blood poisoning.

Delayed Departure

Dr. Leach delayed his departure eastward to care for the wounded man, amputated his arm, saw him recover, and found himself involved in the fortunes of the county. What he did likely amazed even the doctor himself. His surgical instruments had been either lost or stolen on his journey to California, and he had no better option than to perform the amputation with a wood saw and jackknife, and no anesthetic.

The doctor joined the Mariposa Battalion under Major James D. Savage as a private. Within two weeks he was the battalion surgeon and had improvised a hospital on the Fresno River, with the only materials of poles, willow matting, and green brush.

When the four-month war operation was over and peace was restored, Leach formed a partnership with Savage and his partners in the trading posts along the river country. He and Savage had become good friends. Leach became manager of the store on the Fresno River.

Store was Opened

A branch store was opened at Fort Miller and in his comings and goings, Dr. Leach took care of the sick people at Millerton. In December 1860, during the winter flood, the doctor became water bound at Millerton for six weeks. He decided not to return to the Fresno River area. He disposed of the stock in the store and took up his life in the county seat of the new county of Fresno. Henceforth, his life was bound up with the people at Millerton and, later, with the town of Fresno.

Dr. Leach saw the beginning and the end of Millerton. When the county seat was removed to Fresno in October 1874, he was the last official to leave Millerton. He made the trip with the patients in Russell Fleming's stages.

The hospital in Fresno was established in rented quarters. The doctor became as prominent in the new town as he had been in Millerton, both medically and as a citizen.

Whenever a new enterprise was suggested, the citizens turned to Dr. Leach for consultation, and he was usually the sponsor.

Headed First Bank

Vandor records that Dr. Leach

fathered the first water works with the pumping plant so long located on Fresno Street ... [and] was president of it until 1890 and sold it for $140,000. He was president of the first bank in Fresno, a private enterprise in one of the early brick houses on the north side of Mariposa midway between H and I, and of which Otto Froelich was the cashier. He was an organizer of the Bank of Fresno and its president until it went out of business on account of the provisions of the new constitution of 1879 regarding stockholders' liabilities for indebtedness; an organizer and president of the Farmers' Bank; fathered the gas company; was identified with the first electric light company and the first streetcar company with the fairgrounds as its terminus and was one of the promoters of the fair association with its races and agricultural exhibitions.

It was during Dr. Leach's long service to the county that the first county hospital was erected.

The doctor had been a bachelor for forty-two years when he married Mathilda Converse, the widow of Charles P. Converse in 1872. Converse had constructed the courthouse at Millerton.

'Dignified Bearing'

The doctor and his wife made an imposing impression; he had a dignified bearing, straight-back pompadour and beard (both white in his later years). His wife was vivacious and charming. He always dressed well, according to a columnist of the 1930s:

> Although the fastidious doctor seldom wore the tall silk hat so popular with later accessions to the profession in Fresno, his jewelry and clothing were elegant to the extreme. His wife, who had beauty and graceful, charming ways, was notable as well for her jewels and laces and brocades. She drove a fine horse with satiny brown coat and sweeping mane and tail to a canopy-top basket phaeton but was usually alone.

They both painted oils, and the doctor was a rather good violinist, but rarely played publicly. He had a passion for fine horses.

The collapse of the boom made inroads of the Leach fortunes.

Resigned in 1893

Dr. Leach resigned as county physician in 1893 at the age of seventy, after thirty years of service. He went back into private practice and served nearly to the last day of his life. When he died in March 1897, his funeral was the largest that had been accorded to anyone in Fresno before since the settlers arrived.

A detailed study of Dr. Leach's life would see him in many poses. Hardly anything of worthwhile importance that happened in the county did not show his name in some capacity—director, trustee, sponsor, or friend.

Mrs. Leach died in 1919. They are both interred in Mountain View cemetery.

Chapter 31:
Major Savage

The life and adventures of Major James D. Savage of early Mariposa and Fresno Counties have been the basis for a number of volumes devoted to historic Fresno. With his family, he meandered westward from New York to Illinois. He married his childhood sweetheart in 1844, and two years later they took off for California with their baby daughter.

The hardships were too much for the wife and child, and the young adventurer left them in unmarked graves along the westward trail.

Savage reached Sutter's Fort in the fall of 1846. He let no stone remain unturned to further his fortune in those violent and disturbing years of the California province when it first became annexed to the United States. Although some historians claim Savage was in the Bear Flag Rebellion, his name is not listed in the inexact records of the muster roll.

Dissatisfied and Rebellious

However, we do know with certainty that he was a member of the Fremont California Battalion. It is recorded in histories of those times that he was a dissatisfied and rebellious person. Yet all descriptions that have come down the years concerning the man show him to have been a man of great and attractive personality. One trait stands out largely: he was able to make friends with the Indigenous people and influence them in all matters.

This influence particularly manifested in his ability to engage them to work for him and to manipulate them to be content to turn over all the gold they found in the Southern Mines to him, for which they were paid (for their daily labor and finds) in blankets, clothing, and food, plus the trinkets they adored.

His time spent in the Battalion served a good purpose to Savage, as he became very familiar with the country. From his Indigenous friends, he learned of the Valley of the Tulares.

The lakes, swamps, and sloughs that made up the Tulares made travel unpleasant for newcomers. The physical makeup of the country made it possible for hiding places for renegades and deserters—from both the Indigenous and civic-religious factions of the frontier. This mixture of humanity brought nothing good to the Indigenous people of the Tulares.

Attracted Many

However, Tulare Valley possessed enough natural beauty and resources to attract many people. There was plenty of animal life for food and skins. On top of all these natural advantages, there was James Savage with his alluring personality and his ability to know what was coming. His sense of future happenings seemed as good as his leadership. He held them "in the hollow of his hands."

In the middle 1840s, the Indigenous people were restless in all parts of the San Joaquin Valley. One reason for this situation was the rapid state of affairs that caused changes in government. For a time, there was no way of having any department of law on hand to use authority, or to make laws concerning settlement.

Another reason for so much lawlessness was the influx of eighty thousand immigrants coming through the area in 1894. The pathway through the San Joaquin Valley to the Mother Lode country brought many along the hill road south. This began to crowd the Indigenous people from their territory. The Indigenous people began to target those who were traveling and settlements. A military camp was established at Taylor's Ferry on the Stanislaus River where the river leaves the foothills.

Minor Role

The first notice given historically concerning Savage and his spot in the Battalion was on the march from Monterey, November 17, 1846. His role in the conquest of California is a very minor one. But his affiliation with the Indigenous peoples and their cultural norms, as well as their loyalty to him personally, not only did something materially for Savage but had its imprint on the civilization of the great valley where he had cast his fortunes and life.

He became a chief of several different tribes. He married Indigenous women and worked up a personal friendship with Jose Jaurez, the chief of the Chowchilla tribe. His Indigenous friends began to call him El Rey Huero, the Blond King. Savage was so delighted with his title that he assumed all the rights and privileges of a king. His friends became his subjects. His spoken word was a command.

Savage also let it be known that he preferred the title El Rey Tulares.

Gave Presents

During this new regime of his, Savage set up a trading post on the south fork of the Merced River. From his vantage point at the post, the new monarch gave presents to his subjects, but they had to present him with the shining gravel they had found. Savage's income increased. He did not forget the presents, and they became greater too. The king and his empire were happy.

The Tulare empire spanned from the Mariposa country to the north to the King's River to the south. All the Indigenous people in the Tulare region were on good terms with Savage, but those in the hills did not return his fealty.

The Grizzlies, or the Yosemite tribe, were especially hostile to Savage, although at times they visited his trading post.

Life was not pleasant for the new king's subjects. The gold rush had wiped out all order in California. The land of the Tulare was overrun by men who coveted gold ore. There was plenty of it, for El Rey Tulares ruled a land that was in the center of a great gold-producing region.

The mad rush for the hidden wealth in the soil harmed the Indigenous people; they were losing their lands and their rights. James Savage realized the situation. He was equal to the need of the moment. But his solution to the trouble brought only criticism to the blond king of the Tulares.

Savage's Relationships

The combined activities of his mines, his stores, and the Indigenous people made Savage an impressive character in the frontier days of the valley. His operation brought him into close contact with other men with whom he was associated in mining ventures. The Indigenous people of Tulare began to resent his association with the White men. This, in addition to the animosity of the Indigenous people who lived in the hills, began to bring trouble.

In the spring of 1850, Savage's wives informed him that the Indigenous people were planning to drive the White people off their lands.

The first raid was made upon Savage's trading post on the Merced River. Following the raid, Savage moved his post to the Mariposa River at the junction with the Agua Fria Creek and also established a branch on the Fresno River.

In October of that year, he made a trip to San Francisco for supplies and to store his gold. He took many Indigenous people with him to impress upon them the power of the White man.

Knocked Down

One member of Savage's party, Jose Juarez, became intoxicated rather than impressed, and was knocked down in a quarrel with Savage.

On the way home, Savage learned of trouble up and down the valley, and hurried to his Fresno River post since it was more vulnerable to attacks than the other post.

He found a large gathering at the trading post and attempted to persuade them of the folly it would be to try to drive the White men away, as they were stronger and could kill them.

Savage did not get the same reaction as he had when he had played the role of king to them. He asked the quarrelsome Jose Juarez to repeat what he had said to them—that the White men would kill them all. To Savage's amazement, Jose Juarez contradicted everything that Savage had said.

Savage hurried to his Mariposa post where he talked with the Indigenous sub-agent concerning raid possibilities. The White men with whom they talked seemed to feel the raids were not serious. The agent was not worried. Savage felt he could handle them if he could talk with them.

Something Was Wrong

One December day, no Indigenous people came to the post at all, causing Savage to wonder. By nightfall he was certain something was wrong, especially as even those with whom he had connections had disappeared.

Savage and a few companions started out. About thirty miles from his Mariposa post, he saw a large group of Indigenous people across a canyon. They informed Savage there had been a raid on the Fresno River post and the clerks had been killed. The Indigenous people from his town refused to go back with him; they said they were tired of working in the mines and were going to drive the White men out. They told Savage they would spare him if he left them alone.

Savage and the agent found the Fresno River post a shambles. The three clerks had been killed. The store was looted, and the cattle stolen.

James Burney, sheriff of Mariposa County, raised a company of seventy-four White men who went against the Indigenous early in January of 1851. The White men won the battle but made such a poor showing that the Indigenous people were encouraged. Burney wrote the governor for help, detailing all the raids and battles and the numbers killed, which included seventy-two men on a raid at Rattlesnake Gulch.

Hero Worship

Many of the company were young, venturesome men. They were so impressed with Savage that after they attacked a rancheria, they turned to hero worship. One of the men expressed his views about Savage in a letter:

> From his long experience with the Indians, Mr. Savage had learned their ways so thoroughly that they cannot deceive him. He has been one of their greatest chiefs and speaks their language as well as they can. No dog can follow a trail like he can. No horse endures half as much. He sleeps but little, can go days without food and can run a hundred miles in a day and night over the mountains and then sit and laugh for hours over a campfire as fresh and lively as if he had been just taking a little walk for exercise.

The efforts of Sheriff Burney and the Indigenous agent met with varied results. The commander of the U.S. troops on the Pacific Coast thought his force was not strong enough to be effective. The Secretary of War told the governor of California that only the President of the United State could call out the militia.

Since it was traditional that the frontiersmen of California were the best equipped to resolve conflicts with Indigenous warriors, Governor John

McDougal issued an order for the creation of a volunteer group to be known as the Mariposa Battalion.

Jim Savage was made commanding major of the battalion when it was mustered in at Agua Fria in February 1851. The muster roll of the battalion had 204 men listed. They were divided into three companies.

Raids continued. Commissioners toured the areas, seeking to defeat the Ahwahnechee and Chowchillas Indigenous peoples. They burned down Indigenous villages, destroyed their food, and entered into treaties, some of which would be broken.

The Mariposa Battalion was phased out on July 1, 1851. Major Savage went back to his trading activities.

Forced Relocation of Indigenous People

California was still in its infant years as a state when the conflicts with Indigenous people increased. The settlers decided to force the Indigenous people to relocate to reservations, as they thought that would increase safety for the settler citizens. A commission was established to negotiate treaties with the various tribes. The treaty Commission was composed of George Barbour, Redick McKee and Dr. Oliver Wozencroft. The commission members were Easterners, so they were not as knowledgeable of the ways and languages of the Indigenous people as were the Californian settlers, who were, for the most part, men of immediate action.

When some of the tribes refused to come in for peace talks, Major Savage was placed in charge of a battalion to search for them and persuade them to surrender for talks and life on a reservation.

Chief Tanaya, leader of the Yosemites, one of the largest and strongest tribes, was a chief resister.

Set up Camp

Savage set up a camp on the Merced River. This camp was named Camp Bishop in honor of a man who had fallen into the icy waters of a creek the previous day. Savage sent Indigenous runners to inform the nearby tribes that it would be wise if they came of their own accord and agreed to sign treaties as other tribes had done.

One of the runners was sent to acquaint the chief of the Yosemites with this order. On March 23rd, Tenaya appeared at the edge of the camp and waited to be asked to enter. He was suspicious at first, but after being fed and treated well, he agreed to take the word back to his tribe.

Tenaya was back the next day to tell Savage his people were willing to move to a reservation, but that it would take some time before they could be there. It took time to pack their possessions, and since the trails were deep with snow the women and children would not be able to travel fast. This explanation seemed reasonable to the commander of the battalion, and they waited for the rest of the tribe to appear.

When the Yosemites failed to show up the next day, Savage expected some trickery from Tenaya. By the middle of the morning on the 25th, the troops set out for the village. They found it difficult traveling as they ascended the divide to the east of Camp Bishop. In the middle of the afternoon, they came upon seventy-two of the Yosemites. Tenaya said this was all that would come; the rest had fled to the Tuolomne area and the Mono Country. Savage did not believe Tenaya, knowing that there should be more than two hundred in the tribe. He sent Tenaya back to camp with the seventy-two others under guard.

Savage and his men started out on the clearly marked trail the Indigenous people had so recently made.

In a little more than an hour's march, Savage and his men reached a promontory in the vicinity of Old Inspiration Point. It was from this spot, directly across from El Capitan, late in the afternoon of March 25, 1851, that the full glory of the lovely valley was seen.

It was because of his position as commander of the battalion that Savage was given the credit of discovering Yosemite Valley for the settlers.

It fell to Dr. Lafayette Bunnell, a member of the battalion, to give a name to the valley. Sitting around a campfire that night at the foot of Bridal Veil Falls, the subject of a name came up. A number of names were suggested, but Dr. Bunnell insisted that the valley should be named for the tribe that had called it their homeland.

These White men were not aware that the valley already had a lovely sounding name by the Ahwahnee: the Deep Grassy Valley. The name Tenaya was also used as a place name in the valley.

Dr. Bunnell later wrote:

> It seemed to me that I had entered God's holiest temple, where were assembled all that was divine in material creation. For days afterwards I could only think of the magnificence, beauty, and grace of the waterfalls, and the mountain scenery; and an almost total lack of appreciation of the event on the part of Major Savage caused me to think him utterly devoid of sentiment.

There seems to be no mention made in history of any personal effect upon Savage of the beauty of the valley. He was intent only on getting the Indigenous people removed and settled on reservations, and then returning to his trading posts.

Further search for the rest of the Yosemites was made the next day but they found no more. They returned to Camp Bishop, assembled the rest of the battalion, the pack animals, and the captive Indians and returned to the Fresno River region where headquarters had been set up.

Expeditions were sent out later to explore the high Sierra country, including the Yosemite area. Many currently well-known peaks, lakes and waterfalls were discovered and named by the settlers. Savage himself never returned to the valley he had discovered. He kept busy with the Commission as an interpreter and trying to negotiate relations with the Indigenous people. By the time the Battalion was mustered out, all the tribes had signed treaties and had gone to live on designated reservations on the Fresno and Kings Rivers.

Savage was then free to return to his own affairs.

Dr. Bunnell's great impression of the finding of the valley still lives in history with more of his graphic words:

> It has been said that it is not easy to describe in words the precise impressions which objects make upon us. I cannot describe how completely I realize this truth. None but those who have visited this most wonderful valley can even imagine the feelings with which I looked upon the view that was there presented. The grandeur of the scene was softened by the haze that hung over the valley, light as gossamer, and by the clouds which partially dimmed the higher cliffs and mountains. This obscurity of vision but increased the awe with which I beheld it, and, as I looked, a peculiarly exalted sensation seemed to fill my whole being, and I found my eyes in tears with emotion.

When the Major hurried him for fear of potential violence, Bunnell replied, "If my hair is now required, I can depart in peace, for I have seen the power and glory of a Supreme Being; the majesty of his handiwork is in that Testimony of the Rocks."

Savage's Store

After the Mariposa Battalion disbanded on July 1, 1851, Major Savage lost no time in getting back into his business of storekeeping. He opened a store on the Fresno River near Coarsegold, having already arranged for a license to act as a trader with the Indigenous people. It cost Savage $1,200 to secure the license. The Mariposa-Agua Fria store was re-opened at the old location.

The Fresno River store became a busy place. Things were so prosperous that Savage built another post called Fort Bishop, near the Fresno reservation. Savage and his partners, Dr. Lewis Leach and L. D. Vinsonhaler, were doing very well financially.

Savage, being a licensed trader, had the privilege to petition the government for reclaiming losses he had sustained in December 1850 from a raid. He put in a claim for $25,150, but never received any returns.

Historians differ as to the status of Savage's wives after the war between the Indigenous people and settlers was over. In fact, they differ on the number of his Indigenous wives. He is credited with having from two to seven wives.

Savage's Friendships

Following the war, Savage regained the friendliness of the Indigenous peoples. Although Savage became prosperous throughout his career and used them, it is often believed that he was their friend.

Due to his prosperity and the monopoly he had on trade with Indigenous people, Savage received the enmity of the White men who were coming into the area.

The impact of new settlers into Mariposa County along with the continuing conflicts brought about the creation of a new county. This new county, Tulare County, covered 24,231 square miles. It was bounded on the west by the Coast Range, on the east by the Utah Territory, on the north by Mariposa County, and on the south by Los Angeles County. Fresno County had not as yet established.

July 10, 1852 had been set for the election date for choosing officers. Savage had been appointed to head the commission for the election.

Some of the White men, due to their great jealousy regarding Savage's prosperity, claimed he had negotiated the treaties and secured excellent land for Indigenous people for his own ends.

Led Attack

One of these men was Major Walter H. Harvey. Harvey was elected judge of the new county, although he had led an attack on some peaceful Indigenous people eight days before. Their "crime" had been only to protest the presence of squatters near their homes.

Savage had supported Harvey because of his military abilities, thinking they would be an asset to his position. Harvey's attack on the Indigenous people only moved them to travel beyond their home limits to trade with Savage rather than with Harvey, who was a trader as well as elected judge. Savage had pacified them, but it was too late to do anything about Harvey being elected to office.

The hostility between the two traders increased. Harvey is said to have remarked that Savage was "no gentleman." He accused Savage of cowardice and duplicity in his dealings. All this went from "bad to worse."

Having occasion to go to a large gathering of the Indigenous people of the Kings River district, which was called for on August 20, 1852, he stopped at the store at Campbell's Ferry on the morning of August 16 and asked for Major Harvey, whom he seemed to know was there.

Fight Started

Savage took this opportunity to tell Harvey that his attack was to be investigated and advised him to turn himself in. Harvey agreed to do so. As Savage turned to leave, he reminded Harvey that he knew of his remarks about him and asked him to retract them. Harvey refused. A hand-to-hand fight started, during which Savage's pistol fell from his waistband. Savage's friend, John G. Martin (who had served in the Battalion as quartermaster) was with Savage and picked up his pistol. Before Savage could regain his pistol, Harvey had shot him. Savage died instantly.

Savage's death was a sensation. He had been a public citizen in his work among the Indigenous people. The newspapers of the state expressed regret about his death, for it was felt that Savage could do more to keep the Indigenous people in line than all the treaties or agencies.

Eyewitness Account

Annie R. Mitchell, author of a history of Savage's career, documented this eyewitness account of what followed Savage's death:

> The night he was buried, the Indians built large fires around which they danced, singing the mournful death chant until the hills around rang with the sound. I have never seen such a profound manifestation of grief. The young men, as they whirled wildly and distractedly in the dance, shouted the name of their Father that was gone, while the squaws sat rocking their bodies to and fro, chanting their mournful dirges until the very blood within one curdled at the scene.

E. F. Beale, Superintendent of Indian Affairs in California, called Savage's death a sad calamity, saying "he was a benefactor in his limited sphere; his place will long remain unoccupied."

Harvey stood trial in Tulare County for the murder of Savage. The trial was apparently a farce. Harvey, as county judge, had to appoint someone as justice of the peace for the investigation of the case. He appointed a close friend of his, Joel H. Brooks. The appointee took the testimony of several witnesses, all of which were friends of Harvey. Brooks then dismissed the case.

Savage Monument at the grave of Major James D. Savage, located south of his old trading post on the shores of Hensley Lake in Madera County, California. (S. Bybyk)

No Record

There seems to be no record of Harvey acting as judge of Tulare County, but there is proof that he did hold the office for two months and eighteen days, receiving a county warrant for $213.70.

Harvey's future was not a dim or harassed one. He was a member of the posse that allegedly captured Joaquin Murietta. In 1854 he was appointed sergeant-at-arms of the California Senate, and in 1859 he married Miss Helen Downey, whose father became governor of California from 1861-1862. In 1861 Harvey was appointed Superintendent of Immigration of the port of San Francisco, a post he held until his death in August 1861.

A few years after Savage's death in 1852, Dr. Lewis Leach, his friend and former partner in business, had Savage's remains removed to the Fresno River area, near his old store in 1855. Savage's grave is by a ten-foot monument made of Connecticut stone. The monument was shipped from Connecticut by water to mark his grave in a "rock-bound bed in the middle of the stream."

In 1974, Lake Hensley was created by way of the construction of Hidden Dam on the Fresno River. Savage's monument and grave were moved to a hill on the shores of Hensley Lake in Madera County, California.

Chapter 32:
Railroads

From the time the Central Pacific Railroad came into the San Joaquin Valley, a number of small railroads were built. Some were independent roads, while others were branches of the Central Pacific, later to become known as the Southern Pacific. These small railways extended here and there to join the valley centers with a main line.

There was one small railroad that generated a lot of hopes and brought some glamour as it branched out of the City of Fresno.

This railroad, and the building of it, is the story of Marcus Pollasky, who came to the valley as a so-called agent of East Coast capitalists. Pollasky was honest enough about the fact that he was sent to Fresno as an agent of capitalists, but he wasn't quite transparent about who really sent him to woo the Fresno City and County people for a railroad project.

Pollasky told the people that he represented capitalists who were attracted by the wealth, high class, and power of Fresno's citizens and that they wanted to do something about the neglected resources of the mountain country of the county, meaning the vast forest of the Sierra.

Every Trait

Pollasky seemed to possess every trait of personality that was to persuade people to listen and to heed any plan he should desire to undertake. He proved to be a highly skilled salesman. He was "personable, versatile, magnetic, and freehanded."

A few years before Pollasky's arrival in the valley in 1891, the citizens experienced a land speculation. The dreaded time of ebbing prosperity could happen, and there were those who wanted to reach out for anything that would keep disaster away.

The way to this proposed mountain wealth, Pollasky said, was by way of a railroad into the mountains. The great forests, Pollasky said, were neglected resources. Fresno could assist in his idea and plans. The way was simple: grant a right of way to the San Joaquin River. If the citizens of Fresno would do that, the capitalists would cover all other expenses for building a railroad into the mountains.

The results would be startling. The wealth of the wooded area would come to Fresno; there would also be an easy method of transportation into the wonders of the high region, granting relief from the miserable hot summers and bringing the joys of the skyland in the other seasons for recreation.

Willing and Ready

Pollasky was indeed persuasive. A number of the leading promoters of Fresno were willing and ready. Pollasky was made the lion of the hour; he was wined and dined. He became an honorary member of the National Guard. Private conferences were held with him. The men of capital, the realtors, and the corporation lawyers rallied around him. Pollasky, in turn, never failed to enact his charm for them.

There were also those who opposed his plans. The opposing faction claimed that Pollasky was in a crooked game. He wasn't sincere. Many were sure that the Southern Pacific had something to do with Pollasky's scheme.

Pollasky had plenty of money to push his project. He bought an entire block of land in the city and built a magnificent home on it. That turned the tide in his favor. If he had faith enough in his own plans to become a resident and citizen of the county seat town, he must be pretty sure of results. Consequently, many people contributed money toward the right of way to the river.

Opportunists Won

The supporters and detractors went at it, each side fighting for its opinions and actions to play out. The opportunists won. One of the leaders of property and action in the county was Thomas E. Hughes. In collaboration with Fulton G. Berry and John D. Gray, two other upstanding and progressive men, Hughes took the lead in paving the way for the railroad for Pollasky.

The three men agreed to raise $100,000 to purchase rights of way, provided that a hundred miles of would be built, fully constructed in every way, and thoroughly equipped and maintained.

On July 4th, a big celebration inaugurated the work.

Hughes made a speech and promised the people that "three years from today 1,000 towboats will be used to transport your products to tide water. Three years from today you will have two other railroads running through your city competing for your patronage. Ten years from today your imports will be, instead of $10,000,000, increased to $50,000,000 and the end not yet estimated."

This sounded like an Erie Canal might be brought to the County.

Hughes turned the first few shovelfuls of dirt and the brass band played.

Glad Hand

As time went by, plans did not go smoothly, but Pollasky, keeping himself in the limelight, would not let interest in the railway lag. He continued to mingle among the people of Fresno, turning on the charm and giving a glad hand to everyone concerned.

An imposing depot was built at the eastern end of Tulare Street, and interest boomed higher.

By late autumn the road was nearly finished to the river where there was a settlement called Hamptonville, named for W. R. Hampton who had land on the Fresno side of the river and had built a store and hotel. Pollasky purchased the Hampton land and buildings, and the town was renamed Pollasky.

Winchell gives November 25, 1891 as the date that the railroad reached the site of Pollasky (erstwhile Hamptonville) about twenty-five miles from Fresno City. Invitations had been sent to those concerned with the right of way and their influential friends for another big day of celebration. A long line of passenger coaches, and several flat cars with improvised sets of lumber, left the Southern Pacific depot in Fresno, carrying several hundred people for the trip to the rail terminus.

Another Speech

Hughes made another speech, and Pollasky, Judge E. C. Winchell, and Judge C. A. Hart all talked to the crowd. A barbecue dinner was served on long tables inside tents.

On January 20, 1892, the road was opened for traffic. Southern Pacific engines and cars were operated by Southern Pacific crews. The fears of the opposing faction had materialized.

Pollasky left the area and sold his mansion, leaving a disillusioned populace.

The 100-mile railroad was never completed. The town of Pollasky became officially Friant in 1907.

The Southern Pacific absorbed the railroad to cut off competition. The wrath of the people lasted for years, and the experience served as a block to any projected railway enterprise in the county.

Essential Transportation

The expansion of a settled area depends upon transportation. Before the days of the automobile and the airways, the railroad was the fastest and most well-rounded of any method of transportation. Fresno County must give credit to the Southern Pacific Railroad for the county's fabulous speed of growth in population and industry.

When the Espee (which stood for "S. P.," a nickname for Southern Pacific) failed to satisfy the settlers in the San Joaquin Valley with rate charges sufficiently reasonable to patronize it for freight traffic, there was protest. The protest ended in tragedy, which left a mark of darkness on the history of the valley.

The great valley that was to become a heartland for the greatest need of humanity—food—was then withering on its own vines because of the inability to export its great crops, which were great in both quality and quantity.

The rivers of the valley had made possible the production of ample fruits and vegetables that could feed the people of the state of California and other areas. All that production would be worthless if the commodities from the land could not be sold. If no profit could be realized from the crops, the settlers could not hold onto their lands.

Need for Imports

There was a need to receive imports into the valley as well as to export farm products. Both imports and exports were necessary for the valley's subsistence as a farming region, as well as the progress of the state. Every commonwealth worth its food rations had to progress in ways of living other than raising food for itself and its neighbors.

Something had to be done about the railroad monopoly in northern California if the valley were to continue to exist as farmland. San Francisco merchants were as worried as the valley farmers about the situation.

The Santa Fe Railroad was on its way westward and fought for a way into California over its own tracks. It was the dream of Cyrus K. Holliday, founder of the Santa Fe Railroad, to link Chicago with San Francisco by rail.

Rumors and Facts

Freighting troubles continued, and there were rumors and facts that caused troubles in addition to freight rates. There was a threat of freighting the California grain crop to the Gulf of Mexico for water shipment. There was also the threat of shipping from Mexico to Hawaii, which would doom San Francisco trade. In 1891, a British ship sailed into San Francisco with cargo consigned to a San Francisco merchant. This cargo ship had been routed from New York to Belgium to California. The cost of such shipments was less than shipping across the nation by land.

It cost more to ship goods from San Francisco to the San Joaquin Valley than to make the same shipments three thousand miles across the nation from North Atlantic ports.

The troubles were bound to come to a head, and they did.

Leaders Met

San Francisco merchants and leaders met to consider building a railroad for San Francisco and the valley.

On January 22, 1895, two score of these interested men met at the Chamber of Commerce to discuss the issues involved. Isaac Upham, in calling for the meeting, wrote as follows:

> Some of our friends feel quite discouraged, but I for one do not feel like giving up the fight yet. We should continue to work for at least 30 days longer. We should submit this matter to real estate owners, merchants and everyone who is interested in the prosperity of this City and if they say 'no, we will not

subscribe', the failure is not our fault, and the blame must rest on those who refuse.

The meeting brought results. Attendees included leading merchants, capitalists, and men of affairs, including Claus Spreckels, the sugar magnate.

Took the Floor

When Upham timidly suggested that it would take $350,000 to initiate the starting of a people's railroad from Stockton to Bakersfield, Spreckels took the floor.

"You are not fighting a little concern," he told them. "You're fighting a big one, a rich one, and one that will fight back. You talk of $350,000. That's nothing. Make it 3,000,000 and I'll put myself down for $50,000 right now." Spreckels' energy carried the day. Two of those at the gathering immediately offered $5,000 each for the cause.

Spreckel's two sons, John D. and Adolph B, each offered $100,000. Two others put up $50,000 each.

The San Francisco Savings Union also gave $50,000. James D. Phelan, Jim Flood, Joe Donohue, and the Hearst Estate gave $25,000 each. There were smaller pledges from various Anti-Monopoly Clubs.

Railway Organized

By a month later, on February 20, within the timeframe suggested by Upham for making the effort, the contributions amounted to $2,248.000. The San Francisco & San Joaquin Valley Railway was organized. The railway directors were Claus Spreckels, W. F. Whittier, Charles Holbrook, John T. Doyle, and E. F. Preston.

All the valley towns celebrated the victory. Fresno, Stockton, Santa Clara, San Jose and Bakersfield fired cannons, listened to bands play, and held torchlight parades to show their reaction to the coming of the people's railroad. Here was good old American competition. The people's railroad. That's what it was called: The People's Railroad.

Many people bought stock in the company. Others offered land for rights-of-way and depots.

Instead of going back to an uninhabited desert, the valley took heart; it had hopes now instead of discouragement and wasted crops.

The story would not be finished until the rails were laid. But the new spirit—the spirit that had brought American settlers to Pacific shores—would truly save the day.

William Storey and the New Railroad

The directors of the proposed line, the San Francisco & San Joaquin Valley Railroad, lost no time in getting down to the business of organization. Articles of incorporation were filed five days after the historic organizational meeting held on February 20, 1895. The projected transportation system would usher in competition that would be useful to the state, the valley, and the County of Fresno.

All the people of the great valley, which had originally taken up a third of the State of California, had a new material hope to cling to for their personal advancement as well as the progress of their commonwealth.

William B. Storey, Jr., a native Californian, was appointed chief engineer for constructing the new railroad. He was born in 1857 in San Francisco, which was then still a gold rush town. He worked his way through school. After he left college, he went up to Idaho and over to Wyoming and Utah to do survey work for the Central Pacific Railway.

Storey came to the new railroad little realizing he would one day become president and the subsequent owner of the Santa Fe Railway.

Helped SP

He had helped in the construction of the Southern Pacific in the Sacramento River region and into the northern part of the state. All that experience would be invaluable for the building of the Valley Road.

Storey began his survey work for the SF&SJV in April 1895, starting at Stockton, the northern gateway of the southern half of the great valley, the San Joaquin.

Stockton, some seventy miles east of Oakland, was then a town of 20,000 people. People commuted between the town of Stockton and the city of San Francisco on passenger ships. Barges carried freight cargo between the two points.

The great plains country in the valley had always produced some form of food—cattle, grain, and later fruits and vegetables—that could make or break the valley economically, depending on methods of transportation.

That was why Stockton put up $125,000 to aid in the building of Spreckels' enthusiastic dream, supplemented by land. Spreckels never for an hour relented in his interests and activities for the building of a rail line into the Valley. When fundraising was at a low point, he subscribed $500,000 in response.

Develop Flats

Spreckels went to the state Legislature and obtained the right to develop some mud flats known as China Basin in San Francisco for a terminal there. Oakland contributed $187,350 and San Jose added $65,000.

The San Francisco *Examiner* ran subscription blanks and submitted some to all the workingmen's clubs, hopeful for more share-buying.

Two thousand pounds of the necessary size of rails, paid for in cash, were shipped out from New York on the steamship Washtenaw, which sailed into Stockton in July of that year. Sometime later, 10,000 more pounds came in two windjammers through the Golden Gate Construction work that started that summer. Contracts for grading and bridgebuilding had been awarded. The line went steadily south toward Fresno.

New towns sprang up along the valley course ahead of the line. Escalon was the first. Irrigation projects were started. The valley folks were going to be ready for the new iron horse.

'The Emancipator'

The valley railroad became known as "The People's Railroad" as it stood in their minds as "for the good of the people." At times it was jokingly called the Emancipator.

On October 5, 1896, the new train took off on its maiden trip, starting at 8:07 a.m. This first train was hauled by a great Baldwin engine, and John Armstrong was the first engineer. The train consisted of six new coaches and two combination passenger-baggage cars. The engine, very new, hit the road at a mile a minute. It was gaily decorated with ropes of colorful flowers, and the brass work glittered as it drove through the California autumn morning.

There was joy in the valley that day as dreams came true once more via a transportation vehicle. Thousands of people lined the railroad's course, collectively feeling that this speeding instrument would again change the valley into new Elysian Fields.

Unscheduled stops were made along the route so that the Valleyites could inspect the cars and the shining engine. Even the engineer was in a gay mood that day and waved at the celebrants.

The passengers were in a carnival mood, and many wore badges that read "Stockton Rejoices with Fresno."

Southern Pacific Railroad Depot, located in downtown Fresno at Tulare and H Streets as it looked in 1900. It was constructed entirely of brick and topped with a slate bellcast hip roof in the Queen Anne style. Construction began in 1889 to replace the small wooden structure that had been established in 1872. (S. Bybyk)

'Ready to Ship'

The engineer brought his great iron steed into the Fresno station at 1:30 p.m. Full farm wagons stood near the tracks, symbolic of future shipping products. They bore placards proclaiming, "Ready to Ship on the Valley Road."

The line construction into Fresno was completed on the very day of the entrance of the train.

The town went wild. It was all set for a gala day. Girls, lovely in white dresses made in the latest fashions, rode in the grand parade that extended for a mile in length. They held a bright banner proclaiming the main issue of the moment. Stylishly dressed women held their parasols to protect them from the warm California sun as they stood with their families to watch the parade or rode in fringe-topped buggies in the procession. It was a truly festive day.

Professional men, merchants, and day laborers were lined up along the line of the parade march.

Following the conclusion of the parade, the populace enjoyed a big barbecue of meats, bread and cups of coffee. Tons of the best grapes of the Valley were piled on the tables for the crowd's consumption. There were many nighttime events including a banquet and entertainment.

The forty-year-old county had gained more stature. The twenty-three-year-old little city had come of age—again!

Cyrus Holliday

Cyrus K. Holliday founded the Santa Fe Railroad in 1859 and became its first president in 1860, vowing that he would one day link Chicago with San Francisco. It was more than a vow; it was a prophecy. Holliday had come into the national transportation picture when he went from Pennsylvania to Kansas in 1854. He was intrigued with the railroad building that was unfolding all over the country and eventually got into the thick of it himself. He was a graduate lawyer and found it easy to write railroad charters.

It was the old Santa Fe Trail that engendered the idea that Holliday visualized: using the old trail for modern and faster transportation across the country, from Kansas City to Santa Fe.

The Conquistadores

He thought of the days of the Conquistadores of Spain and the riches they represented—embroidered shawls, bright feathers of tropical birds, laces, wines, silks, sugar. He thought of the hordes of people moving slowly westward, with ox teams hauling their covered wagons, pushing handcarts as they walked, seeking better fortunes.

He thought of the traders who carried gold, fur, hides, and colorful fabrics from eastern mills. He thought mostly of the faster transportation a railroad would provide.

"Trains will beat wagons," he said, "We can haul freight for half a quarter of the present rates. There'll be new settlements all along the line."

The route was talked about through years of war and through dreadful years of drought. Eventually, Holliday finally saw his rail system take shape.

Great Moment

When the San Francisco and San Joaquin Valley Railroad was completed to Fresno, it was a great moment for Fresno County. In May 1897, the line reached Hanford, thirty miles down the line. By September 9 of that year, the line had reached Visalia, and by May of 1898, it had extended to Bakersfield.

Chief engineer William Storey had made several survey routes across the Tehachapi Mountains, blocking the way south. All the routes would have meant expensive construction. The Southern Pacific had already utilized the shortest practicable line over the twisting mountain grades.

The Valley Road extended on from Bakersfield to Kern Junction. The two railroads agreed to use the Southern Pacific's line over the fifty-eight miles of mountains between Kern and Mojave.

At Mojave, the Valley train took off on the Santa Fe toward Needles on the line it had leased from the Southern Pacific. This gave the Santa Fe a complete connection between Chicago and Stockton, about seventy miles away from the goal of Holliday's dream and prophecy.

Only Waterways

Up at Stockton, there were only waterways to get to San Francisco.

There were problems to overcome to reach San Francisco. There were ten miles of tule swamps and two mountain ranges that stood in those seventy-seven miles.

The track was built across the swamp by steam shovels with clamshell buckets. An embankment was made on the ten-mile swamp. They let it settle and built more on top of it. They fought slides and washouts, but in the end, they had a strong and stable foundation for a track. It took a year to build that embankment over the tule swamp.

The next barrier was through unstable coastal hills through which they finally made the Franklin Tunnel, working against the odds of ground that moved constantly and had to be held back and strengthened with masonry work.

Only the Waters

The northern extension of the Valley Road was completed to Richmond by July of 1900. Only the waters of San Francisco Bay stood in the way of completing the transportation system.

The railroad was prepared with its navy.

Ready and waiting for this moment was a wooden-hulled, paddle-wheel ferry ship named *Ocean Wave*, the last link in connecting Chicago with San Francisco. The little steamer was 180 feet long, with a twenty-nine-foot molded beam and a registered depth of nine feet. The ship was designed by Jacob Kamm and built in 1891 in Portland, Oregon. Fifty staterooms on the main deck and a hundred on the upper deck were luxuriously furnished.

On that July morning, the *Ocean Wave* stood in its ferry slip in San Francisco, newly painted, polished and wearing the emblem of the Santa Fe Railroad. The proud little ship bobbed energetically while the 250 passengers got aboard. It was cheered by two thousand well-wishers who lined the wharf.

Rang Bells

Forty minutes later, the *Ocean Wave* reached Richmond, and the passengers were transferred to a train. The engineers of the ship and the train rang their bells and whistled. The train passed through the Franklin Tunnel, out over the tule swamp area on the new embankment, on to Stockton and down the valley south.

A few hours later, another train at Stockton sailed on toward San Francisco Bay with fifty passengers who had entrained at Chicago for San Francisco, the first to make the connected trip from the Windy City of the Prairie State to the City of the Golden Gate.

The Ocean Wave served regularly until it was placed in retirement in 1911. It was not to be scrapped, but was purchased to serve as a receiving ship for the Sea Training Service during World War I. After the war was over, it was bought by a restaurant owner. As the years began to show on the proud little bay steamer, it faded from the scene.

Other Steamers

There were two other ferry steamers that plied the waters of the bay, assisting in Santa Fe's little navy. They were the *San Pedro* and the *San Pablo*, serving regularly until they met their fate. The *San Pablo* was scrapped. The *San Pedro* was sold for operation at the World's Fair at Treasure Island in 1939 and 1940.

The valley railroad had achieved the purpose of its inception. It was purchased by the Santa Fe Railway, which paid the actual cost of construction and equipment.

The valley was now served by two railway systems. Fresno County, along with the rest of the great valley, would reap the rewards of the advantages of the facilities and would continue to expand and progress.

Cyrus Holliday died that year. His old railroad buddies would no longer chuckle and smile, a mix of tender and joking, about the railroad that Holliday had talked about for so very many years. His dream had been realized and they cheered him wholeheartedly.

Storey stayed on as chief engineer of the Santa Fe and went on to become president of the railroad.

Chapter 33:
Fresno Land Grant

There were very few Spanish land grants in the San Joaquin Valley. Of the seven grants fully or partially in the valley, there were only two that had any part in the history of Fresno County: the Santa Rita, for the most part situated in Merced County, but which was partly in Fresno County, and the Laguna de Tache y Limantour, which was entirely in Fresno County.

The Santa Rita was granted to Francisco Soberanes. This was a large tract, well-watered by the San Joaquin River and the several sloughs that intersected the river. The grant, fully titled El Rancho Sanjon de Santa Rita, contained 48,824 acres. The grant was applied for in 1841 but was not confirmed until late in the year 1862. Sub-divisions of this rancho were later acquired, gradually, by Miller and Lux.

Manuel Castro, a former Army captain, was interested in a fine timbered tract in the delta of the Kings River. The grant, given to him by Governor Pio Pico in 1846, was in the middle of the great valley, with the soil made rich by overflow from the Kings River.

Lived in Monterey

Castro never lived on his ranch, instead living among his friends in Monterey. His grant had come effortlessly to him, and he considered it a source of money. He soon began borrowing large amounts from keen American money lenders. He mortgaged his land at the rate of three percent per month, compounded monthly. He also deeded parts of his land. He deeded to Jeremiah Clarke, among others, two undivided Spanish leagues for ten thousand dollars.

When the US land commissioners made their investigation of the Castro grant, they had to reject his claim because of the many inconsistencies in the title.

But Castro went right on deeding his land away and borrowing more money. In one instance, Castro borrowed $3,500, giving a note and mortgage for one year with interest at five percent per month, payable in advance monthly.

Castro appealed his case and finally received the title to the land. The instrument was recorded in the first volume of Fresno County patents on March 6, 1866.

The property description for eleven leagues reads: "bounded on the south by the Laguna de Tache y Liman-tour (Summit Lake, the only little lake in the vicinity;) on the north by the Rancho de las Hotantos (a rancheria of an Indian tribe;) on the west by the Sanjon (slough) de San Jose, and on the east by the plains."

The eastern boundary was almost unlimited; it certainly was an elastic border for Castro.

Care of most of Castro's land fell to Jeremiah Clarke, who had always been too ready to oblige the grantee.

The happy life of the caballeros of the Mexican rule made them easy prey to the greedy, crafty gringos.

In August 1866, less than half a year after confirmation of the title to the land, the Castro family disposed of all the remaining rights of the desirable land in the delta that comprised more than forty-eight thousand acres to Benjamin Lathrop for the sum of fifteen hundred dollars.

Owners Followed

There were multiple successive owners in the wake of the Castros. Fortunes were made and lost over the de Tache. Speculations ran rampant over the unique boundary lines given so freely by a governor to a friend; at that time, a few leagues were of little concern. The romance of a famous grant that lay wholly in Fresno County passed from the picture.

With the cutting up of the vast acreage, the face of things changed. Each new owner took what they wanted in one way or another, helped along easily by the unconcerned Castro. By their own reckless generosity, many grantees became separated from their wealth and their lands. A later owner stocked the land with cattle.

Another later owner came from Scotland, and another was a firm in London. A canal and irrigation company had possession of it at one time. There were individuals and partners, rentals and sales. The story of the Laguna de Tache y Limantour was a dream of "human hopes and sorrows."

Chapter 34:
Tollhouse and the Academy

Tollhouse, an early small settlement, is situated at the foot of Pine Ridge. The climb mountainward at this point is steep and laborious in every aspect. The site, which is thirty-five miles northeast of Fresno, is sometimes spoken of as Toll Road or Toll Gate and has a history that goes back long before the San Joaquin Valley plains were settled and viewed as inhabitable by Europeans. It is worth acknowledging that Indigenous peoples are believed to have been living in this region for over thirteen thousand years.

Before the 1860s, a lone seeker of new lands appeared in this area along the banks of Big Dry Creek. Elijah Sarver was the first settler in the area.

Sarver brought with him a flock of goats. He built a shelter for himself, and protective fences for his goats from wildlife. Sarver remained only until 1866, but a mountain bears his name.

Into this setting, which was explored and settled, came many people attracted by the vigorous work in the lumber industry. The teamsters somehow made the ascent and descent of hazardous trails up and into the mountains.

The Town of Tollhouse, located at the foot of the Tollhouse Grade, was a key lumber depot and shipping point for the mills on Pine Ridge. (S. Bybyk)

Among Newcomers

Among the newcomers to Tollhouse in 1868 was C. A. Yancy and his family. He found work hauling lumber and opened a hotel. On May 8, 1876, Tollhouse became an official post office.

The native tree life and sawmills continued to flourish as time went on; the community and its local names never completely died out.

Settlers coming to the region found it a good place to reside. They were not far from the county seat at Millerton, and the winding road could take them to Visalia, Stockton, and north. It was considered a route of least resistance. The settlements along the Kings River, especially Scottsburg (later known as Centerville), could be easily reached. It seems that most roads, uncharted or otherwise, led to the Tollhouse region and its take-off climb to the higher country and the rich resources that had never failed.

Fine Ideas

The settlers had fine ideas about making the region a community. A school was one of their first efforts. A small, crude building was constructed for a schoolhouse. Lizzie Ellis, a daughter of the county superintendent of schools, was employed as teacher. The parents of school children gave consideration to homesites and built their houses as close to the school as they could.

Miss Ellis did not teach for very long. She married A. J. Thorne, who in 1874 became county treasurer. A young physician, Edward F. Greenleaf, took over the work of teaching.

In the fall of 1870, James D. Collins, who had been teaching over in the Kings River country, came to the Tollhouse area with his young wife and took over the role of teacher, doing a very fine job.

Around the center of this area, Section 14, Township 12, S., Range 22 E., J. G. Simpson donated ten acres of land as his part of community affairs. Others subscribed to the fund, giving sums from $250 to $750 and more for the construction of a new schoolhouse.

Cost of the Schoolhouse

The lumber building was erected in 1872 at a cost of about six thousand dollars with Thomas Whitlock as master builder. The site upon which the settlers built the schoolhouse was a beautiful grove of oaks, facing the high road. There were two large rooms in the building and a shady veranda was added. The windows were tall, and every item of school equipment available at that time was provided for the use of the children.

The arranging of classes and grades was a bit unorthodox, and each pupil progressed according to their own will and ability.

"The Academy" was established in 1872 in Tollhouse, CA. It was the first secondary school in Fresno County. Originally, it had side porches that were removed in 1882. (S. Bybyk)

Under Collins, it was possible to absorb knowledge from the higher branches of learning, and the school was aptly, and proudly, considered an academy. The building soon inherited the name spelled with a capital "A," and they were very proud of it.

The older building was used for various purposes, but later the Academy served as a church until a building for religious services was erected a bit further up the road.

Families Moved

When Fresno became the county seat, many families from the higher region transferred their work and homes down onto the plains. In the following years, the road was changed, and the fine schoolhouse was left far back from the newer thoroughfare.

The district drew less school money and the once treasured building fell into disrepair and turned gray, losing itself in the grayness of the oak trees.

A later member of the early Simpson family caused the old roadway to be changed, and starting in 1920, the wandering trail that had led to so many attractive spots in the hills was wiped out.

The venerable hall of learning, so much enjoyed by the first settlers, was finally torn down, and a more modern one was constructed in a new location.

Progress continued, and nothing stood still. The old area came along with the times, moving forward along with the rest of Fresno County.

Chapter 35:
William Faymonville

There is never enough space in any narrative series to include the complete history of every public-minded and useful person within a community. Now and then, one stands out as sufficiently eminent to preclude any ignoring of activities, interests, and actions that have supported the public good.

Such a person must be acknowledged; it is historically important that the name and work should be recorded. There is honor in being the first mayor of a municipality, even without the title.

The person accorded this distinction in the city of Fresno was William Faymonville.

Faymonville spins many threads through the fabric of the history of both the county and city of Fresno. A pioneer of Millerton, he emerges from the early years of the county with many noteworthy roles and contributions.

Historian Paul Vandor places him in 1851 as a member of the election board in Texas Flat (Coarse Gold Gulch) precinct as clerk. If Vandor is correct in the year, then Faymonville was then working under the auspices of Mariposa County, as in 1851 there was no Fresno County. It is possible that 1851 is an incorrect date.

Flashes Through

From then on, he flashes through Fresno history—a service here, a social contribution there, a county official, a businessman, a politician, a homebuilder, a city and county builder. His entire career, he was somebody that was never left out of the general running of affairs.

He served as a county official from 1861 to 1871, first as assessor, appointed to fill an uncompleted term, and then as county clerk, auditor, recorder, and public administrator. Some of these offices were combined. In the beginning, the county clerk was also recorder and auditor, with the roles being separated later.

Faymonville was one of the last to leave Millerton for the new county seat town. His office was torn down along with other buildings of the town for the hegira to the new location. He was also a partner in the Millerton Ferry Company, located below the town of Millerton at Rancheria Flat.

Use of Dust

In writing concerning the use of gold dust as the coin of the realm, in the early history of Millerton, Vandor records that a notice was in the newspaper: "On and after the 1st of March 1865, we, the undersigned, pledge ourselves to receive and pay out GOLD DUST at the following rates only," and there follows the names of the mining locations and the monetary value at certain rates per ounce.

The final paragraph reads: "The above rates are as near as we can come at the value of the various kinds of dust in gold coin, and after this date, we do not intend to receive or pay out anything that is not equal in value to United States gold or silver coin."

Faymonville's name is one among the thirty-four signers, with all names occurring often throughout the pioneer history of the region.

In 1870, Faymonville presented the editor of the *Expositor* with all the ten issues of the *Times*, the first newspaper of the county. J.W. Ferguson, the newspaper editor, bound these with his first year's issues of the *Expositor*. When Ferguson died, the complete file of the two news sheets came into the possession of Edward Schwarz, a "bibliophile and curiosity collector," as the historian commented.

There has been very little documented concerning the family of Faymonville—no mention of parents or where he hailed from. One comment may lead one to believe he came from a European country.

Established Bank

According to the Vandor history, Faymonville, Otto Froelich, Dr. Lewis Leach and Charles H. Garth established the first Fresno County bank. The banking firm went under the name of Garth and Froelich and was housed in a small brick building on Mariposa Street, near I Street.

In 1875 William was in the Abstract business in Fresno County, but by all accounts was already a political force in the County of Fresno. He was on the payroll of the huge Miller and Lux company and advised them on who to back for county positions. While still on the Miller and Lux payroll, he was appointed Deputy Assessor for Fresno County. Later, he was Clerk and Recorder for the county.

Not lacking in cultural contributions to the community, Faymonville also served as an official in the Fresno Social and Literary Club that was formed in 1876. He sang in the choir on the day of the laying of the cornerstone of the new courthouse in Fresno City.

After the incorporation of the town of Fresno in 1885, Faymonville, as chairman of the first board of trustees, was in essence the first mayor. The title of mayor was not given to the office until 1901 when the City Charter was approved by the state Legislature. L. O. Stephens was the first to carry the civic title of mayor. For all of these years in Fresno, Faymonville operated without the title of mayor.

Along with many others who profited from the great land boom in the late 1880s, Faymonville made a great deal of money, and as others did, he built a beautiful home. The house was located on four lots at the northwest corner of Van Ness and Stanislaus Streets. His family included his wife and a son from a former marriage.

The house, for all its beauty and charm, was conservative. It had eight rooms, was two stories, and had an attic, a basement, high ceilings, and tall windows. Just as the house was nearly finished, its master became very ill. When it was ready for occupancy, and things were favorable for moving Mr. Faymonville, his friends took him to his new home and got him settled in a comfortable room upstairs. His time in the new home was short.

Less than a year after his death, his widow remarried to Bailey K. Leach, a newspaper man, promoter, and adventurer. After some time, both the estimated property of one hundred thousand dollars and Leach vanished. The widow was left with her older son and two small children fathered by Leach to get along as best she could.

Chapter 36:
Early Religious Services

During the first years of Millerton, there was little thought given to religious services. Life was wild and rough there on the banks of the river where miners came to find gold. There was never a resident minister of any faith, and no church edifice was every built. When ministers of the gospel came to the area, they were given respect due to their calling. Many of them were known as "circuit riders," and held meetings in homes. Historian Winchell records, "It is probable that the first regular minister in this region was a Methodist circuit rider named David Latimer, who established a following, first at Millerton and then at Scottsburg, in 1854."

Paul Vandor earlier recorded, "At great intervals, mass was held on stated church festival days, with a clergyman sent for the occasion from Visalia for the benefit of those of the Catholic faith at Millerton."

The first recorded religious service held in Fresno County took place on October 21, 1855 and was conducted by the Reverend William Ingraham Kip.

First Bishop

Reverend Kip had been appointed as the first bishop of the Episcopal missionary district of California a couple of years prior. He was a member of an early family of settlers in New York and had studied law before entering the ministry. He left the post of rector of St. Peter's Church in Albany, New York to take on his western assignment.

The minister was forty-two years old and at the beginning of a fine career in New York when he left for California. He was the author of multiple books and was known as a scholar, a minister, and lover of culture. His friends were somewhat surprised at his new and unexpected plans. His background did not lead them to understand his decision to go into a pioneering capacity in the Far West.

His wife and son came west with him to his new headquarters in San Francisco. His new diocese extended eight hundred miles from north to south, and between two hundred and two hundred and fifty miles from east to west. This vast area was broken up by valleys, mountains, and rivers.

The bishop made plans to visit the isolated river area on the San Joaquin while on a tour that took him to Los Angeles. He left the southern community on October 8, 1855, his party being escorted by Major E. A. Townsend and a troop of soldiers who had been ordered to inspect both Fort Tejon in what is now Kern County and Fort Miller in Fresno County.

Adventurous Trip

The bishop's party had traveled south on the steamer *Republic* from San Francisco. They left Los Angeles in a vehicle drawn by four mules. After an adventurous trip, they reached Fort Tejon on October 11th, and services were held there in an unfinished barracks the next day. By the 19th they reached Four Creeks where they encountered many Indigenous people.

The bishop wrote in his report: "Before us stretched a plain, scorched, dry, and apparently boundless, without a tree for miles. ... By mid-day the sun was burning hot, and we dragged ourselves over wastes of sand 'til our animals dropped, and we ourselves were almost exhausted."

The bishop and members of his party took turns riding and walking. They camped by the Tule River, where they refreshed themselves with a bath and spent the night with a settler and his family. They pushed on to a grove of oaks in the Visalia vicinity, camping on the Kaweah River.

When the group reached Millerton, they paused for a brief rest before going on to the fort. Later he wrote of the hill town: "It consists of some 20 houses, most of them of canvas, two or three being shops and the majority of the rest drinking saloons and billiard rooms." Although it was Sunday, the bishop noted that "the population on this day seemed to be given up entirely to dissipation."

Sighted Fort

They sighted the fort around eleven that morning on a plateau a half mile upstream from the banks of the river at Millerton.

At that time the complement of the fort numbered approximately seventy enlisted men and officers.

That evening, church services were held in a large room in the officer's quarters. All the officers attended the meeting and most of the men. Following his scripture reading, the bishop bapitzed the baby daughter of a soldier, Private Hugh Carroll.

The bishop and his party remained at the fort for ten days. He took the stage to Snelling in Merced County and Stockton and returned from there to San Francisco by riverboat.

Before he left, he licensed the fort surgeon, Dr. Murray, as a lay reader and arrangements were made for regular Sunday services. On October 21st in 1920, sixty-five years later to the very day, a number of Episcopal clergymen and friends traveled to Millerton to honor the anniversary of the bishop's services at the historic spot.

Bishop Kip–Fort Miller Memorial overlooking Lake Millerton. (S. Bybyk)

It seems that the regular services might not have been continued. Columnist Ernestine Winchell records in a series that six years after Bishop Kip's stay at Fort Miller, there were no services there.

Monument

On the 12th of May, 1957, a four-ton monument of Fresno County native granite was removed from the Academy area to a high spot above Lake Millerton and inscribed to honor Bishop Kip's memory. The stone is unpolished; it was left in that state intentionally, and the inscription was sand blasted onto it. The inscription reads:

> Commemorating the Centennial of the first recorded religious service in the Fresno area, performed at Fort Miller on Sunday, October 21, 1855, by the first Protestant Episcopal Bishop of California, the Right Reverend William Ingrahm Kip. Dedicated to those of all faiths who have propagated religion in this area since that day.

In May 1861, another clergyman came to the area through the ministrations of the Catholic Church of Southern California. Father Daniel Dade was sent to the new parish in Visalia. He was also a recent addition to the state, having come west from Philadelphia.

Father Dade fell ill from malaria and decided to spend some time in the higher altitude of Fort Miller, thinking it might help him to recover his health. While there, he lived at the fort and found people of his faith to attend to him. Before he returned to his parish, he had mingled with the people of the area and found many ways of assisting them. After his return to Visalia, he did not forget the little hill community. He returned every spring to spend time with them, making the trip by horse-and-buggy, carrying with him his vestments and linens, the sacramental bread, and wine and silver.

Father Dade was of Irish ancestry and had been blessed with a genial manner and much wit. He was universally popular, as much with the rougher element as with the people of higher status. There were several families in the old Fresno County seat town who were able to appreciate his learning and enjoyed entertaining him in their homes during his stay.

In the saloons and gambling places, he was received with courtesy. On one occasion all the dust and coins on the table were given to him. When someone asked him if he "would use that dirty money," he replied that it would be blessed by the good it would do.

Through the spring of 1872, he continued the visits. In the fall of that year, he retired to a monastery in Sacramento, where he died a few years later.

Chapter 37:
Cattle Kings

When Fresno County was still a part of Mother Mariposa, it was a cattle paradise. When the miners began drifting into the hill country along the San Joaquin and the Kings Rivers, they found cattle roaming and grazing with the elk and antelopes. Before the California missions became secularized, great herds of horses and cattle grazed on the territory adjacent and tributary to the missions. It was part of the occupational plans of the established missions to build up agricultural pursuits with gardens, fruit and shade trees, as well as droves of stock; all this was for food as well as a way to train the Indigenous peoples in the ways of the White man.

Cattle drifted from the mission areas, as did the Indigenous people trying to make a new life away from the harsh treatment of the settlers. They took stray animals when they had the opportunity. When the settlers first entered the valley, there were thousands upon thousands of the wild mission stock.

Looked Good

It looked good to the newcomers: horses for riding and work; cattle for meat, hides and tallow for commerce; garden food; and water for every purpose.

The cattle from the mission were not from such fine breeds as Jerseys and Herefords. An early chronicler described them as "wide-horned, thin-hipped, fleet-footed and savage creatures built for strength and endurance and spotted and streaked in endless variety of design."

As settlers came to the region, either to work in the mines or to follow agricultural pursuits, many brought their own "bossy cows" behind the slow-moving covered wagons. Some of the incoming people drove small herds with them westward. The progeny of these increased as time went by.

Early in the county's settlement, great numbers of cattle were driven up from New Mexico, Arizona, and Texas through the Los Angeles trail northward. These cattle were the founders of Fresno County's later great herds.

Cattle Kings

It was over that southern route that pioneers William Hazelton, John Patterson and Jefferson James brought their bands in the 1860s to the Fresno Plains. For about twenty years, these men were the cattle kings of the county and adjacent territory. They drove their stock to San Francisco, Stockton, and Sacramento for marketing.

In 1864, Tom Hildreth, who had acquired the old Santa Rita Rancho (once a Spanish grant), sold his vast acres to the upcoming Miller and Lux corporations. The Santa Rita Rancho lies in the land that bounded Dos Palos and Los Banos.

Tom Hildreth was the oldest son of ten children who came with their parents from Missouri to California. As the family settled here and there, Tom took up cattle raising. His herds flourished on the rich well-watered Santa

Rita land. When he sold the ranch to Miller and Lux after a very dry year, the property was the first land purchased by Miller and Lux.

The brand of the Santa Rita Rancho originated with the Hildreths. Their mark, which stood for the Hildreth brothers, was a combined double "H" made by three vertical bars crossed in the center by one horizontal bar. It went with the ranch to the purchaser and was used by them from that time on.

No Boundaries

In those days the cattle range knew no boundaries. The stock brands, which were required by law to be recorded, identified them for their owners. All disputes pertaining to ownership of cattle were settled on the basis of brands.

The "no fence law," introduced to the legislature by J. W. Ferguson, the editor of the Fresno Expositor and a politician in the legislature, was passed in 1874. The big cattlemen, who ranged their stock wherever they wished, were quite startled at the law. Many of the small farmers had protected their property by wooden fences—back before the invention of barbed wire—to suit their own individual situations.

After the law passed, the cattle barons took their herds to the foothills or out of the state for grazing.

Branding corrals and roundups were part and parcel of the early ranchos, small and big. The roundup was usually an exciting time for the ranchers, their families, and the vaqueros. Grazing cattle, lush grasses, cowboys, rodeos, roundups, branding, cook houses and cook wagons, mustangs, saddles, bridles, spurs, wide-brimmed hats, silver bangles, and the reatas fashioned from rawhide strips—all went to make part of the romanticized west of which Fresno County was a part.

Most Exciting

The settlement and expansion of the "Last Frontier" was possibly the most exciting part of the history of the nation in the last half of the 19th century. The whole westward movement was also spoken of as "the West" or "the Far West," and so it must have seemed like that to many of the weary travelers that came through the plains as they rolled on in their Prairie Schooners, far from the eastern regions.

Not only was the actual movement westward something of great import as they became the first White settlers and pioneers, but there was a great attraction for the life that compelled the writing of histories, fiction stories, drama, and the traditions and legends that followed in the wake of transition.

The cattle era was a great one. History is rife with it from the annals left by land speculators, government officials, the U.S. Army, and the diaries left by old-timers and their descendants.

Chapter 38:
Jefferson James

Jefferson Gilbert James was one of the commanding figures of Fresno County during the early years of the cattle raising and grazing era.

Great as his interests were in both the county and city of Fresno, he never established a home in the region. When Fresno Station was established in 1872 with the entry of the railroad into the Valley, James was the first to ship stock to San Francisco. He built loading chutes along the tracks between Tulare and Kern Streets. Before the railroad came, James, along with other cattlemen of the county, drove cattle to San Francisco. In 1882 he was elected a member of the Board of Supervisors of San Francisco and in 1886 was elected School Director for the city and county of San Francisco. He was the president of the Fresno Loan and Savings Bank of Fresno in 1888.

James operated his own marketing business in San Francisco rather than seeking a separate business for those services.

From his home in Missouri, James followed the Argonauts to California to prospect in the Mother Lode. By 1857 he had made a large enough stake to buy 960 cows, which he drove to the "25" Ranch near Kingston, across the river from where present-day Laton is located. Here he pastured his cows.

Lots of Room

James was a man who needed lots of room to work in, so in the following year, 1858, he took his stock to the Fresno Slough and turned them out to pasture on a vast acreage of forty to sixty thousand acres—historians disagree on the exact acreage—that he had acquired the title to on both sides of the San Joaquin River.

Prosperity shone on the young man from Missouri, and in 1860 he went back to his home state, married Miss Jennie Rector, and brought her to his ranch headquarters at old Fresno City on the Slough, a site now known as Tranquility. James established his home on the coast, but he traveled back and forth to his ranch and home. He and Jennie had one daughter, Maud Strother James, who went on to marry Walker C. Graves. Walter Graves was a prominent lawyer in San Francisco who was a candidate for Attorney General, though he lost the election. After Jennie's death in 1902, James was re-married to Jennie's sister, Elizabeth, in 1903.

A large two-story house was built in old Fresno City. It was painted white and called Casa Blanca. After a great flood, the house was moved from its first location to a new headquarters site several miles east of the Slough, where it was used as a bunkhouse for cattle hands until it burned down.

Friendly Man

By the time Fresno Station became the county seat and found itself well on the way to the status of a city, James had discarded his cowboy type of clothing and the manner of the range, but he was, in the fine days of his opulence, the same genial, friendly man he had ever been. He was called "Jeff" by his friends and acquaintances and returned such friendliness. When in Fresno City on business, he was always a guest in one of the leading hotels.

In the 1880s, James was active in educational affairs, serving as a supervisor and then a director in the San Francisco schools. He was also a director, then president, of the Fresno Loan and Savings Bank.

A railroad crossed the section of the county his land was located in (the West Side) and a station was called Jameson for him.

In time, James was to have trouble with other cattlemen, especially Miller and Lux. The Miller and Lux holdings were mainly across the river from James' land, and they made claims against James for water rights. Vandor records that Henry Miller instituted six suits against James, while James had one against Miller.

Not Personal

It is said that though all the lawsuits and bickering about water rights was bitter, the trouble never became personal. Historian Paul Vandor writes:

> The point whether James could take water from the San Joaquin and the Kings was involved in it all. James' lands did not abut directly on the river but were on the slough and watered by the overflow. He contended that this entitled him to take water from the river above him. ... The decision by the supreme court after long litigation was for James. The decision only precipitated another battle with the San Joaquin and Kings Company which has a contract to take prior water from the river. The point then was whether James had to wait until it could have its 760 cubic feet of water before he could be served with any for his lands. In this suit, the superior court gave judgment for him three days before his death.

When James died at the age of eighty-three in 1910, he was one of the few pioneers who acquired great wealth and then kept it for himself and his family to enjoy. From the beginning of his career in California, James had no significant financial hardships.

At the time of his death, James was reputed to have assets worth more than $1,500,000, part of which was a hundred thousand acres of land. In time some of the land was sold for colony lots and Tranquility became the civic center.

Chapter 39:
Henry Miller

"Miller & Lux" is a combination of names that many people are familiar with. It has meant a great deal of power and wealth. Before there was a Lux in the partnership, there was a Miller. Though Charles Lux was an able man, capable of amassing his own fortune, Henry Miller was the more active part of the partnership.

The story of Henry Miller and his dealings with people, land, and stock is momentous. Henry Miller was born Heinrich Alfred Kreiser, the son of a German village butcher. Before he was eight years old, he was already schooled to herd his father's calves on pastureland, and when not doing that, was learning how cut roasts, steaks, and soap bones. His life was that of the German peasant child—in his case, never really unhappy, but always suffering the poverty of the very low classes.

A Dream

When he was only eight, one day Heinrich had a very active and vivid dream. It was a hot summer day and he had become weary and fallen asleep in the sun. In the dream, which sank deeply into his subconsciousness, he saw an endless region of grasses and fields, and millions of noisy cattle, as far as the eye could see.

One of the vivid pictures that he retained in his memory all his life was the fact that every one of those roaming, bawling animals had an odd mark on the left hip. The mark appeared to be an H and had a blurred H at that. It seemed to be a double H, with three vertical lines that had one horizontal line crossing the three vertical lines.

When the boy awakened, he pondered sleepily over the blurred H. H must have been meant for Heinrich, but why a double one? He supposed it was because he was weary and the noise of the cattle was bothering him, even in the dream.

Starting His Trip

When he was fifteen, he announced that he wanted to go to America to seek fortune. He was tired of poverty. He waited until he was eighteen, after the death of his mother, and then he went to England where he worked for a couple of years, getting together his fare to go to New York.

His life was rough for a time in the New World, but he managed to work until he had the opportunity to take off for California.

He had met a friend whose name was Henry Miller. Miller had planned to go to California and had his ticket purchased to go, exacting a promise from young Heinrich that he would also save his money and join him in California. Soon after, Miller changed his mind about making the trip and Heinnch bought the ticket from him, discovering that it was made out in the name of Henry Miller and was not transferable. The German youth became Henry Miller and retained the name for the rest of his life.

In fifteen years, the new Henry Miller was influential enough to persuade the State Legislature of California to pass a special act to legally change his name to Miller.

He went to California by way of the Isthmus of Panama, experiencing a long layover there. During that time, he took advantage of the illness from fever of the local butcher and made a small reputation for himself for cutting good meat and being honest in his dealings.

San Francisco

He reached San Francisco with very little money left from his small New York savings, but he met many people of every walk of life. He met enough of the solid type of men he wished to befriend and learned of the new country he was going to. He heard of the vast plains and fields of the valleys, the large herds of cattle, and the gold rush area.

Miller had no thought for the mines. He was interested only in cattle and a job. He had no trouble finding work quickly in San Francisco, working in a butcher shop. After a couple of years, he had his own business. By getting up early and getting to the markets first, he had his choice of stock. This helped to add to his fine reputation in the butcher business.

Buying Cattle

A couple of years after he went into business, he was able to pay thirty-three thousand dollars for three hundred fine animals. These animals came from the first band of American cattle ever driven into San Francisco.

This was the beginning of the development of American cattle, "which was destined to crowd out the Mexican cattle, with which up to that time the Spanish rancheros had supplied the market," wrote Edward F. Treadwell in his book about Miller, *The Cattle King: A Dramatized Biography*.

One day when Miller was sorting some hides that were ready for tanning, he noticed the outline of the mark and to his surprise, it was the double H mark of his long-ago dream. Investigation of the brand brought him the news that it came from a ranch over in the San Joaquin Valley owned by the Hildreth family.

The outcome was a trip to the valley and the subsequent purchase of the great Santa Rita ranch. He went home to the city owning over eight thousand acres of land and 7,500 head of cattle.

Building an Empire

He had started the empire he would build. Little by little he acquired more land through both lawful ways and every other way he could.

He knew the land; he knew the soil. He knew the cattle and markets. He bought from the government and from the railroad. He homesteaded and he bought up homestead relinquishments. He bought school land and swamp land. As his lands extended, so did the double H brands on the left hips of his cattle.

The story of Henry Miller and of the Muller & Lux partnership is too momentous to tell here. The concern is mainly to record what this vast Miller & Lux empire had to do with Fresno County.

Local Holdings

After his partner died in 1877, Henry Miller continued to add to his vast acreage. His holdings spread into four Pacific states. When he died in 1919, his estate in Fresno County alone was estimated to be around 268,092 acres. Miller was always happiest when riding behind droves of cattle.

He knew his large estates well and was very observant. There was one incident worth telling that will give the reader an idea of how he worked. He was out at one of his ranches, talking to the foreman. It was a fine-looking ranch, but Miller found some criticisms everywhere he and his foreman went on the ranch tour. There needed to be some wire netting to keep flies out of the house. Pitchforks were placed with the prongs on the floor. This called for some advice on keeping implements covered. The fire wagon wasn't in the most convenient place for handy use. The vegetable garden wasn't big enough for the number of men. The alfalfa was planted too soon after plowing the land. The troughs hadn't been cleaned out. Hogs shouldn't be allowed to eat figs off the ground.

Miller's driver chided him for being severe with his foreman. He told him, "I never saw that place looking so well. Weren't you a bit hard on him?" Miller said, "Yes, the place looked fine. But how long would it stay that way if I didn't keep after them?"

He was a fine organizer and built up a vast estate, which was tied up in litigation for many years. Henry Miller was married twice. His first wife died early in their married years. He married again later and had three children, two girls and a boy. The boy was disabled and died young, and one of his daughters was thrown from a horse and killed.

It was said Henry Miller never called any of his help by their given names. They were always "Mr." Neither did any of his employees call him "Henry." It was always "Mr. Miller."

Chapter 40:
Fresno Scraper

A single piece of farm and construction machinery, invented and manufactured in the late 1880s, practically revolutionized the construction industry and sped up the agricultural progress of the San Joaquin Valley. That implement, which took shape in the minds of men, was born of sheer necessity in the young county, and still younger town, of Fresno.

This implement, which caused such a fundamental change in industries and locations, was an ordinary dirt scraper. It is possible that, with the exception of irrigation and the railroad, it was the greatest force in the advancement of the vast plains of Central California. It contributed greatly to the making of the great heartland of the West—the San Joaquin Valley. Its use was to go much farther than the valley it was designed to cultivate.

The new implement, evolved from the old through need and experimentation, was named the "fresno scraper," and was always to be used as a common noun, being spelt with a small "f." The word "scraper" was never needed for identification; it was named, of course, from the locality in which it was dreamed, designed, tested, manufactured and used: that strange, appealing Spanish word that meant "ash tree." It took the name of its birthplace with it over land and sea, into South Africa, Syria, India, Japan and Russia. It was used on practically every railroad line built in this country. It was used in building the Panama Canal. It was indeed a ditch digger of great proportions—physically and abstractly. But it was always simply a fresno.

Became Farmers

By the time the short-lived mining boom of Fresno County had passed into history, the settlers were, for the most part, farmers who had migrated to California from many sections of the United States and from several European countries. As Fresno County's manifest quota of people surged into the San Joaquin Valley, they brought with them the tools of their trades, or had intentions of sending for them when settled.

Back in those eastern and central states where much of the ground was rocky, the old slip scraper was the only implement that was workable. "But its difficulty of operation," wrote the late Wallace Smith in his book, Garden of the Sun: History of the San Joaquin Valley, 1772-1939, "and the vast amount of clear soil to be moved in canal work, caused men to ponder on other ways and means."

In this western state, the settlers found themselves thoroughly involved in the irrigation situation if they were to raise crops. It meant they had to depend on ditches and canals to get the water from the rivers onto the land where the farms would be.

Trying to use the slip scraper for moving large quantities of loose soil was discouraging. The problem prompted a lot of thinking minds to work. The need was so general for a better and a bigger scraper that thoughts seemed to become contagious; the result was a lot of conflict.

The Fresno scraper was invented to fit the special needs for moving great quantities of earth for canal and ditch building in Fresno County's early days. (S. Bybyk)

Many Inventors

Usually, when a construction foreman or farmer had an idea for improvement of the scraper, he had to go to a blacksmith show to have the work done. That is possibly why there were so many alleged inventors of the scraper. Everyone knew what was going on.

Some historians have given credit to a man named Diedrich for its invention. This credit seems to have taken hold because of the published reminiscences of George Otis, who may or may not have been cognizant of the true facts.

During the winter of 1879-1880, Henry Hawn, Clovis Cole, and Stockton Berry obtained contracts for scraping and leveling land in connection with the construction of the Herndon Ditch. They used several hundred horses in the work but found the slip scraper to still be inadequate. First, the contractors had the workmen plow deeply, and then they used a "buck scraper," which had been devised by Hawn. The buck-scraper was formed like a heavy drag with a runner at the end. With this device they were able to move a yard of dirt on each trip.

In the meantime, Abijah McCall, a farmer, inventor, and contractor, put his mind to improving the scraper. He had come to California from New York in 1856. He had already invented the cross-reaches used on the early buckboards—the same as are now used on vineyard trucks.

Began Work

McCall and his son, William, began work on a sheet-iron scraper. After several experiments in sizes and the number of horses, they decided that a five-foot width was suitable for a four-horse team. This design remained in use as long as horses were used.

When McCall was ready to apply for a patent for his scraper, he had to borrow $150 for the fee. This was made possible by Frank Dusy, who was one of the leading figures of early Fresno County, engaged in ranching, canal building and stock-raising. McCall gave Dusy a half interest in the invention.

W. H. Shafer, an early day civil engineer of Fresno County, supervised the construction of hundreds of miles of canals and ditches, and in doing so watched the development of the dirt-scraper. In an interview in later years, he said that the first scraper was originally designed to be eight feet long, but that it proved too large for six horses and too small for eight horses. It was cut to six feet and then five feet, the size of the patented implement.

Shafer went on record as saying that the impression that Diedrich had invented the scraper was possibly due to the fact that McCall had urged Dusy to take the scraper to Diedrich's blacksmith shop to have it cut to size, as Diedrich had better equipment for such work than McCall had.

Different Design

Diedrich, after seeing the newer implement, made one of a different design, and secured a caveat on it, but it did not prove successful and was never manufactured commercially.

The McCall-Dusy patent for the dirt-scraper reads: "Frank Dusy and Abijah McCall have invented an Improvement in a Dirt-Scraper; and we hereby declare the following to be a full, clear, and exact description of what is known as the Fresno Scraper…"

The dirt-scraper was listed as Patent No. 320,055, and was witnessed by William Faymonville and J. W. Coffman, and was dated June 16, 1885.

James Porteous, a native of Scotland, had come to California and established himself in the new town of Fresno as a blacksmith. He felt that with the coming of the railroad, there would be a good future for the area. He, too, watched the experiments to come up with a better scraper, and had made some improvements of his own, although he made no claim for an invention. He later incorporated his improvement ideas.

Frank Dusy had become disgusted with Diedrich's claims of a scraper invention and sold his half interest to Porteous for five thousand dollars.

Sold Rights

After McCall died in 1886, the two sons sold their rights to Porteous for a thousand dollars, receiving five hundred in cash and the balance in farm machinery.

To protect his interests, Porteous bought out Diedrich. Hawn also sold him his rights, although he continued to build wooden scrapers for the next ten years that were never sold commercially.

Porteous' ventures resolved themselves into the "Fresno Agricultural Works." In contrast to his initial start as manufacturing and repairing buggies and wagons, he had one of the largest businesses in the valley. He held forty-two patents on inventions he made throughout the years.

Fame and fortune came to the young man from Scotland, and he lived out his life in the city of Fresno. He married and left a family. Four of his children later resided in the county.

Wallace Smith recorded in his book, *Garden of the Sun: History of the San Joaquin Valley, 1772-1939*, that the "Fresno scraper was destined to become the proud parent of the modern bull-dozer of World War II."

Chapter 41:
Frank Dusy

When Frank Dusy arrived in the San Joaquin Valley in the 1860s, he brought with him an adventurous nature, boundless energy, and an interest in everything about the new country. In the summer of 1866, he drove his two-horse covered wagon into the county seat town of Millerton and became a citizen of the ten-year-old county.

Settling himself immediately, he set up a photographic shop and proceeded to make tin type pictures. As he had traveled over the country, he carried a portable darkroom along with all the other paraphernalia necessary to make full use of his camera. He never dropped this interest. After he quit taking pictures for a livelihood, he carried on with it as a hobby.

Photography alone could not satisfy this man of many interests. A few years after coming to the county he became interested in raising sheep. Other interests he followed throughout his adult life were mining, soldiering, irrigating, promoting, bricklaying and civic organizations.

Dusy was a French-Canadian, born in 1837, and was left an orphan at the age of eight years. Somehow, he moved to New Hampshire; at a very early age he apprenticed himself as a cobbler, and later, got into quarrying.

Came in 1858

He came to California in 1858 and went straight to the Mother Lode, doing quite well in his efforts. He soon turned to his new hobby of photography.

When the Civil War occurred, he became a member of Company H, Third California Volunteers, seeing service in California only. The reason was that there were many secessionists in the state, and there was a need to have troops on hand to discourage any active trouble.

As early as 1864, when Dusy was hunting antelope in the Coast Range mountains, he and his hunting companions discovered a petroleum seepage that resulted in one of the state's earliest oil ventures. The local Yokuts had used the asphalt from the oil seepage to seal and bind their hunting weapons long before the White settlers had come to the Coalinga area in the western part of the county.

Dusy and his hunting mates filed on claims and took samples of the crude oil to Millerton. The find created some excitement, but the interest lasted only a short time as there was little market for petroleum projects at that time.

Staked Claim

Prospecting in the Sierra foothills resulted in Dusy staking a claim to the granite output near Raymond. This did not prove a profitable venture at the time either, though it cost Dusy and his partners considerable expense.

Assisting William Helm, one of the first large sheepmen of early Fresno County, Dusy became interested in establishing his own business. In a short time, Dusy and Helm had sheep grazing all about the divides of the two rivers, Kings and San Joaquin. Dusy was among the first shippers to use the railroad when it came through the Valley.

In his love for mountaineering, Dusy explored a great deal of the Sierra region as he went ahead of his flocks and herders for grazing land. On behalf of the settlers, he discovered many trails, canyons and meadows, usually giving a name to each as he discovered it.

Frank Dusy discovered Tehipite Valley on the middle fork of Kings River. Some years later he went back and took pictures of the lovely valley and dome.

Teunamahne

An interesting story told about Dusy's mountain climbing is about a narrow and precipitous canyon he took his sheep through, possibly the first time sheep had ever entered it. The spot he wished to reach was about 6,000 feet below the 10,870 feet elevation in Simpson Meadows where his camp was located. The site was named Teunamahne, which was Dusy's utterance of the cry the Chinese herders used to get the sheep down the steep trail.

There is a creek in the high country that bears the name of Dinkey Creek. One day Dusy shot a bear in the North Fork region. Dusy's little dog, Dinkey, followed the wounded bear into the brush. With one fell swoop of a big paw, the bear killed the little dog. The stream near which the incident happened was named Dinkey by the little dog's master. It is called that today and is on the maps of the area.

In 1873, Dusy was married to Miss Catherine Ross. About that time, he bought land near Selma and became interested in raising wheat. He also set out a vineyard and became interested in irrigation.

Irrigation Venture

In 1882, Dusy filed on a thousand second-feet of water from the Kings River. He surveyed and staked the Fowler Switch Canal. Troubles arose in the irrigation venture, and Dusy turned again to a new interest.

He looked into possibilities related to the granite discovery he had made years before at Raymond. He was very successful in this venture, contracting to furnish granite for the additions of county courthouse in Fresno in 1892-93. San Francisco interests bought him out and he was financially solid.

He was able now to build a fine new home for his wife. At that time, it was said to be the finest home in the county. His wife did not live long after moving into her lovely new home, dying in 1897 at the age of forty-six or forty-seven.

Produced Fee

Frank Dusy acquired an interest in the large dirt scraper invented and manufactured in Fresno in the late eighties. He acquired his interest by producing the fee for application of the invention, and his name occurs on the invention application along with Abijah McCall. Dusy later sold his interest to James Porteous for five thousand dollars.

After his wife's death, Frank Dusy set out with some other men to look into the situation of the Alaska goldfields. They selected their claims, and Dusy came back with several of the men to California to recruit others for the Alaskan venture.

One hundred men were signed up and a streamer was chartered for the trip north. During the preparations for the return to Alaska, Dusy suffered a stroke from which he never fully recovered. Hard work and too many disappointments in his efforts in life had taken much of his strength, but he was able to get around with a cane as he continued the preparations for the group to go to Alaska. That venture failed, too. He was only sixty when he died in 1898.

Chapter 42:
Water Tower

Few settlements reach the status of a town without a history of fire behind them. When Fresno started upward on its way to a good-sized community, it had very little water for any purpose other than domestic. In its earliest years, it was ten miles to the closest water—the San Joaquin River. Anton Joseph Maassen, who started the first eating place in Fresno across from the first depot, dug Fresno's first well other than the railroad's well and sold water for men and animals.

The earliest domestic wells in town were dug by the pick and shovel method. In time, those who were economically situated to do so installed pumps and windmills on their premises.

Fire Threatens Fresno

Fresno's first fire was on January 11, 1876 and took a drug store, an adjoining office building, and a saloon. Crowds fought valiantly with buckets of water from water barrels and rain ponds along the street and used wet blankets to save the nearby buildings and stop the spread of fire.

The first volunteer fire company had been organized in 1875 with Johnny Boyle as its chief. The only apparatus the company possessed was one

Fresno's first water works tank tower was built in 1877 at the site now used by the Guarantee Savings Building on the Fulton Mall. (S. Bybyk)

chemical hand extinguisher and the ever-handy water buckets. Meetings were held to discuss ways of preserving town property.

Digging of a Well

In July 1876, two large property owners in the central part of town started operation for a water works. A hundred-foot well was dug, and a seven-inch casing was sunk at Fresno Street and the alley between I and J Streets on the north side of Block 71. This was later to be the rear of the Mattei building and then the Guarantee Savings Building on Fulton Mall. A wooden structure housed the steam pump and supported a water tank with a capacity of twenty-seven thousand gallons. That fall, a banquet was given to honor the proprietors in appreciation of their activities.

The tank tower that was built was, for that time, an impressive feature of the town. It was three stories high so it could serve the tallest building in the town.

The ground portion of the structure was square, and the top was flat. It was sided with boards set in a diagonal position. The second story was octagonal in shape and tapered. It, too, was boarded up with lumber set on a slant from corner to corner.

The upper part, which enclosed the wooden tank, held the same lines as the middle, but projected slightly out. In the eight sections, there was a ventilating panel. The roof was pointed, conforming to the angles of the upper walls.

Founding of the Fresno Water Company

In a little less than a year, other Fresno men became enthusiastic about enlarging the project. The Fresno Water Company was formed with a capital stock of twenty thousand dollars. McCulloch and Andrews retained their interests in proportion.

The board of directors of this corporation was made up of names now important to the county's history: J. W. Ferguson, William Faymonville, W. J. Dickey, A. M. Clark, A Goldstein, Lewis Leach, with George Bernhard, Sr. as president, and Lyman Andrews as superintendent.

That same year, a tank with a twelve-thousand-gallon capacity was added to the plants. For some reason, the iron-banded tub was left bare. An engine shed was backed up to the structure. It was not completed as well as the earlier construction.

Designed by George Washington Maher, a Chicago architect, Fresno's new water tower was completed in 1894. It was in constant use until 1963 when the pumping machinery stopped working. (S. Bybyk)

A Fine Water Tower

As time went on, wells were sunk, and better equipment was added. By the end of the 1880s, the water works were not adequate, and a new location was sought. This time, the location was on Fresno and O Streets where a fine, substantial tower building was contracted for and built. It was not completed until 1894. A house of excellent design was built to shelter the pumps and engines. It stands a hundred feet high with a storage capacity of 250,000 gallons.

In 1963, the Water Tower ended its service, but it still stands as a landmark and is very much admired. It is now known as the Old Water Tower and stands tall and graceful, portraying the simple beauty of a past era.

Chapter 43:
The Roeding Story

There can be no one in the city or county of Fresno who is unfamiliar with the name Roeding. The proud name of a beautiful park, it also carries a history of a great industry that helped to push Fresno into the sights of the world. A little backing up into history tells us that George Christian Roeding was born in San Francisco in 1868, about the time the first railroad entered the San Joaquin Valley.

His father, Frederick Christian Roeding, was a native of Hamburg. Germany. His adventurous nature found him in South America when gold was discovered in California. When the news reached him, he took passage to San Francisco, arriving in June 1849. He went to the Mother Lode and tried his hand at mining.

San Francisco appealed to him greatly and he located here. In the ensuing years, his business affairs made him independent, and he retired in 1865. But his retirement did not mean he sat back to do nothing. He became active with the German Savings and Loan Society of San Francisco where he stayed for twenty-five more years.

Meant Nothing

Retirement still meant nothing to him as far as not working was concerned. He turned his energies to developing the San Joaquin Valley, where with several associates he became part owner of eighty thousand acres of land in Fresno County. This was part of a land grant that the United States Government had set aside for founding the University of California and was sold for $1.50 an acre.

When he visited the Fresno area in 1868 with associates, they found no town except little Millerton in the foothills of the San Joaquin River and Centerville near the Kings River.

When the senior Roeding went back to San Francisco he "would not give five cents" an acre for the entire county of Fresno.

The elder Roeding died in 1910, leaving a family of five children, George Christian being the eldest. Young George's life was that of any young man born to wealth and distinction. He was well educated and excelled in painting. He had a great love for the outdoors, which was evident in his sketches.

Founded Nursery

For all his boasting that he would not pay five cents for an acre in Fresno, the elder Roeding founded the Fancher Creek Nurseries in 1883 and began improving a section of land about seven miles east of Fresno. An imposing residence was built, and the acreage was planted into orchards, vineyards, and nursery stock.

The father took young George with him to the valley to learn the nursery business after he graduated from high school, hoping he would later return and enroll in the university.

The venture of the nursery did not do too well.

There was one fruit that both the father and son were especially interested in—the fig. George had no feeling for the venture as far as the mercantile phases were concerned. After three years in the nursery business, his father was ready to give it up. George pleaded with his father to let him carry on for a year.

Paid Debt

Through good salesmanship and careful management, George came to the end of the year with all debts paid and $3,500 in the bank. That ended the father's nagging for the boy to go to college. He was very proud of what George had done and let him know it.

Thus, George Christian Roeding got his start in nursery lines that led into extensive horticultural development.

George always tried to meet demand with supply. He realized that his nursery stock was not adequate, and he traveled over the state for more supplies, in some cases buying complete nursery businesses and having the stock sent to Fresno.

George was always ready to try out anything that was promising.

Many Experiments

He experimented with many kinds of fruits. He had ranches in various parts of the state. He was most interested in the quality of the fruit, but always there was an interest in the beauty of what his trees would give. Some of his experiments took the form of buying fruit ranches that were not thriving and bringing them to better stock through his knowledgeable care.

He experimented significantly with olive culture.

In his work with fruit and nut trees and vines, he became a well-traveled personage. When he could, he brought specimens home with him with which to experiment. George Roeding's connection with the fig industry provided the high point of his career.

This chapter cannot do justice to a topic as large as the fig experiments and expansion. I can only refer you to the 1930 book *George Christian Roeding,*

1868-1928: The Story of California's Leading Nurseryman and Fruit Grower for reading about his interesting and valuable mission.

All experiments to propagate the Smyrna fig in this country were failures. The trees would grow beautifully but when they reached bearing age, the fruit, if there was any, was worthless. The elder Roeding had begun fig experiments as far back as 1886. He became convinced that "no fig trees at that time growing in California yielded a fruit the equal of the imported article."

In 1886 he sent a representative abroad to make observations and investigations of the Smyrna fig culture. It was about that time that he disposed of his fig orchard and nursery to his son, George. It was largely due to George that the Smyrna fig was introduced successfully in this country. Artificial caprification had begun in 1891. A lot of care and a great deal of expense was involved in the experimentation of the fig before results were evident. Finally, an experiment resulted in some success, but the true flavor and other qualities of the foreign fruit were missing.

Imported Fig Wasp

It was conceded that only by the use of the little fig wasp (Blastophaga, grossorum) could there be a successful crop in California. It had to be imported.

The technicalities involved and the prominent names, private and governmental, that assisted in perfecting the culture of the Smyrna fig fill a volume. It was a long road that the Roedings traveled with the fig culture. It took about eighteen years for the completion of the caprification of the fig that became so very successful.

George Christian Roeding, through his valiant efforts, his patience and his great work, made California the world center of figs. There is one significant paragraph from the book dedicated to the memory of George Roeding that I would like to quote:

> In June of 1899 an employee informed Mr. Roeding that he had found seeds in some of the imported Capri figs, which to

him was singular, as he had performed this same work of artificial caprification before but found no seeds. On examination what were apparently seeds were in reality galls containing the insects. Thus, after eighteen years of persistent effort covering the care and cultivation of a fig orchard without any returns whatever; after many long trials and disappointments demanding a faith and a courage given to but few men; often subject to criticism of friends and relations for holding convictions that were beyond realization; the initiative, vision and indomitable faith of George C. Roeding took material form and Smyrna fig culture became an industry of commercial rank in California.

Perhaps the name of Roeding will also be held in affection by the people of Fresno because of the gift by Frederick Christian Roeding and his wife, Marianna, in 1903 of land for a city park. The original gift included seventy-two acres; five years later, forty-seven additional acres were deeded to the city for park expansion. Since then, it has grown. Through the gift of the site and his valuable nursery training and love of plant life, George Christian Roeding did much to add to its beauty.

Chapter 44:
M. Theo Kearney

M. Theo Kearney, an early Fresno County vineyardist and land baron who earned great riches through his knowledge of land values and persistence to his own personal lodestar, was probably the most controversial citizen ever speculated about by Fresno County residents. Any local history without the inclusion of Kearney would not be complete. However, it is not without contention; from the beginning of Kearney's activity in Fresno County up to his death in 1906 and today, even his name has been a matter of dispute.

What kind of man was Kearney? Why should he be considered here? What was there about Kearney, who did probably more than any other single person to set Fresno County on the way to its future, that caused people to vilify and hate him? Why did his business associates (although they never got close to him) respect him and his abilities as a businessman and rancher who had vision and put actual foundations under them? Was it envy because he was a greater man than any other in the expanding days of Fresno's past?

Kearney came out of the big land deals during the boom days when land values in Fresno skyrocketed as one of the richest men.

He owned and sold a great amount of acreage. He managed and developed some of the early colonies that created his own Fruit Vale Estate and showed what could be done with a study of soil and crops. He showed good taste in the way he dressed; the collections of cultural possessions; the home he built; the grand chateau he planned to build; the way he laid out his landscapes; and the great way he tried to show the grape and raisin growers how to manage their products to get the best prices by creating and leading the Raisin Growers Association. And he showed good sense by minding his own business.

But he had a failing that the open-hearted people of Fresno could not understand, and so criticized.

They made fun of his dress. They censured his formality. They just couldn't take his habits that seemed peculiar to them. They thought him a woman-hater. For what reason? Because he had no local women friends and never told them why.

They were personal about their dislike of the man. However, those who associated with him in the cooperative respected and admired him. But many sneered and made fun of his clothes, even in his earshot. They sneered and snubbed him before and after his death.

During his lifetime, he was a man of mystery. When he died, he left behind clues about his life, including photographs, correspondence, business papers and some detailed date books.

While in the Boston area, in the years 1865 and 1866, not a day was omitted in the date book. But in January 1867, the entries stopped. After a two-year gap, another date book began on February 1, 1869, when he arrived in San Francisco, with periodic entries that included trips, meetings, and business dealings. His datebooks continued with sporadic entries until 1903.

Early Life

Rumors held that Kearney said that he was born in Liverpool, England. He always called himself an Englishman and lived up to the figure of an Englishman of high estate.

He was born Martin Theodore to Irish parents in 1842 in Liverpool, England and had a younger brother. The family name was Carney. In 1854, when the family immigrated to America and settled in the Boston area, they changed the spelling of their name to Kearney.

Kearney pronounced his name as though spelled "Car-nee;" Residents, historians, and his contemporaries gave it the sound "Cur-nee." Though many today are cognizant of the proper pronunciation, the latter is used.

Little has been known of Kearney's antecedents, but there have been numerous conjectures about him as a young man, including prior to February 1, 1869, when he stepped off a ship and became a resident of San Francisco.

In his younger days, while a resident of Boston, he was a devotee of the opera, which he often attended with a companion. At some time, he must have become interested in the stage: however, there has been no certainty that he ever took it up either as a hobby or livelihood.

This phase of his life is known because there was, among his possessions when he died, a book on elocution. The possession of this book in itself sets no definite steering to any particular phase in his life.

There have been conjectures that he changed his name. No definite knowledge has ever been found to either support or deny this suspicion. We do find, written on a fly leaf of this book of elocution, the words: "Remember, M. Theo Kearney." As may happen when a young man takes on something new with great visions ahead, could Kearney have been dreaming of a theatrical career and was only setting forth the most appropriate of names to go by? Was it then that he started using the name by which he preferred to be called, M. Theo Kearney? Did the signature come from his full name, Martin Theodore Kearney, and was that the first time he used it?

During his years in Boston, there was no scandal or hint of anything out of the ordinary about his life. A man in San Francisco, at the time of Kearney's death, remarked to a newspaper reporter that "if people understood, they would feel differently about Kearney." This anonymous man knew Kearney in Massachusetts. He also stated that even as a boy, Kearney was industrious and serious about his work (in a box factory) and spent most of his time studying.

He added that everyone prophesized that he (Kearney) would "make his mark in the world." Later, Kearney went into the business of trunk manufacturing.

During this time, Kearney traveled about the New England states. He advanced from town to town the old-fashioned way of traveling from day-to-day by horse carriage.

Not only did Kearney often attend operas several times a week, but he went to church and attended "sociables" and occasionally a ball.

Coming to California

Kearney traveled to California from Boston via the Panama Canal in early 1869. In California, he had a full business and social life that included travels along the coast. He had prior business contacts made in Boston, most notably William Smith Chapman, and came with his own venture capital. Whatever it was that turned the people of Fresno against him, the San Francisco people did not share this negative view. Presumably the city was large, and it was easier to protect his privacy compared to rural Fresno County.

There are indications that his brother lived in Los Angeles and died there in July 1869. From his notes, he sent his father money for a ticket around that time, possibly for his father to come out related to his brother's passing.

In San Francisco, he associated with the Southern Set. We haven't had the opportunity to trace that group, except we know they were "the older." Did that mean the age of the participants, or the older social organization? He was terse in his records.

It was in December 1869 that he was appointed as land agent for the Chapman, San Francisco capitalist. He had purchased his first Fresno County land in 1869, about six weeks after he came to San Francisco. He bought 8,640 acres for $2.50 an acre, paying $8,000 down in cash.

Life in Fresno

When he came to Fresno in approximately 1873, he was a different man. He worked for Fresno and for the growers, calling Fresno home. But he preferred to remain aloof and out of the social life of the town and county. He was tightlipped about his personal affairs, as he had every right to be, but which was not well received by his neighbors. Fresno was a small town, not much more than a village when it became the county seat.

In 1883, Kearney bought 6,800 acres of land to the west and southwest of Fresno, creating the Fruit Vale Estate. He subdivided the land into roughly twenty-acre colony tracts. He had very strict clauses in the contracts to which he adhered to the letter of the law. The section contained the finest soil in the region. When the "Panic of 1893" resulted in stock and commodities market crashes, he had to foreclose mortgages and take many of the parcels back. This created the greatest storm of all in his rural business life. It is difficult to know why some of the small colonist members prospered and others did not.

Looking upon it objectively, he had every right to do as he did. Perhaps if one could explore the individual sales, it would have some better look about it for Kearney. Some colonists may have been religious about their business transactions and others may have been dilatory in their farming and paying. Time and the tide, which has a way of turning lives, cannot always be traced in individual matters. Foreclosing on residents who couldn't pay and taking back the entire land with improvements earned Kearney resentment from the community. He was seen as a cold, ruthless landlord who had little sympathy for the small growers.

When the raisin growers were having trouble selling their products, it was Kearney who came to them with a plan, forming the Raisin Growers Association. They were loath to follow where he led. Eventually they did, and there are many newspaper and agricultural articles that tell of his success in getting the growers organized for better raisin prices. However, when trouble arose, he was blamed.

Although there has been no record of Kearney having any formal schooling, he showed taste in his books, music, and reading materials. Among the many paintings on the walls of his mansion were some of the masterpieces of his time. His house was grandly furnished with furniture from abroad. Kearney loved fine paintings, fine horses (with which he was an expert hand), music, books, land, the creation of growing things, and the aesthetic and fine arts.

He built a fine mansion and lived there in lonely splendor with servants to wait upon him in every way. Yet he only had but two or three guests ever at his table. One was his superintendent, another an architect, and the third a famous actress. He did not go to others' homes or associate socially with anyone, wealthy or otherwise.

Ladies

Why didn't he like the fair sex? Who can say he did not? While he lived in Fresno, to add to the mystery that surrounded him, he had no women servants, and no women were ever invited to the house. Not one ever crossed his threshold. The one exception was the English actress socialite, Lily Langtry, who had a theater engagement at the Barton in Fresno in 1904. He hosted her for lunch one day. After lunch was over, he dropped her off at her hotel. It is possible that he had met her in either San Francisco or in Europe. That was a great day for gossip, as had been the fact he had no women friends in Fresno.

The only insights we have of female companionship came from his time in Boston. From his notebook, sometimes there is a slight explanation of what opera was heard on a certain date. One name only was used for the people he was with. If it were of the feminine gender, there would be the distinction "Miss" or "Mrs," and only rarely was a given name listed. From late 1865 and throughout 1866, the name "Julie" or "Miss Barker" is often noted and in many entries are listed as "Julie & Home."

There is a photograph that was taken in Boston in 1867. Kearney is shown sitting in a chair, dressed fashionably, his left hand resting on his knee.

Leaning confidently against his right is a lovely lady with a patrician face, also well-dressed. The high point of the picture is that on Kearney's left hand is a wedding band, which might lead one to believe the lady was his wife. At the top of the photograph are the words: "Lizzie and M. Theo Kearney." Not, "Lizzie so-and-so and M. Theo Kearney," but written as though they bore the same surname.

His diary entries stopped in 1867 until he left for San Francisco. What happened to those two lost years? Could he have been married to Lizzie and the daily entries were kept in some other form? Or forgotten in the happiness of a honeymoon, and a possible tragic end to the marriage?

What happened to Lizzie when he came to California? Is that a clue to the odd character attributed to him by his Fresno associates? What else made him a man of subsequent wealth, a millionaire vineyardist, and one of the great landowners of the rich Fresno lands, as well as a recluse as far as women were concerned?

Perhaps the crowning mystery of Kearney's life was the empty chair that was placed at his table every meal with a service arranged for the missing guest. If we could solve that one, we might know the history and understand all of Kearney's actions.

Latter Years

When he became wealthy, he formed a habit of spending several months each year in Europe. Pictures and letters left behind illustrate that his life on the European continent was a mixture of business, health, and social life. In Germany, he spent a great deal of his time at health resorts. Kearney's health had been poor due to cardiac trouble for a long time. It is possible that not everyone knew that. But that was the main reason he went to Europe for a part of every year: to get away from the worries of business and the heartbreaking way he was treated in the community he called home.

In Europe, he hobnobbed with the great and the near great. He was welcomed by royal families. This paradoxical man set the heads to shaking when it became known that he associated with the great names of England and the European continent. Photographs found after his death show him in groups of the social elite of Europe. He also found social and business interests in New York.

He came back to the home county with reverberations that he was an illegitimate offspring of one of the ruling houses of European royalty. This must have caused the rumors in Fresno that Kearney was a "remittance man." That latter statement would hardly stand up in argument when he was on the same social plane as the members with whom he was close enough to have his picture made with and it is not likely that he would, as a remittance man, appear in the same social status.

There is an early picture found among his possessions that shows him without the beard he wore in California. In this he is shown with a receding chin, which is unnoticeable when wearing the distinctive Van Dyke. Here, psychologists could help in the situation of Kearney's aloofness when he first came west. The sneers and comments made about Kearney were often made within his presence and hearing purposely. Who could take that bitter pill complacently? They sneered at his fine clothes, his bearing, and his bachelor existence.

Among Kearney's personal belongings was a picture of a member of an English royal family where there is a strong resemblance between a contemporary monarch and Kearney. It is highly possibly that the resemblance is heightened because the two were similarly dressed.

The people of Fresno turned against him. The word-of-mouth history of his life in Fresno is that he was very seclusive in his associations, seldom carrying on conversation with the people of the town and county and never entering into the social life of Fresno. He was so fitting by looks, dress, education, money, and acceptability that it does seem odd that he should have cut himself off from every avenue of human contact in the community he called home.

We know that not only did he accumulate money for himself, but that he was instrumental in making it for the vineyards of every rancher in the county. He left the raisin cooperative after a last great fight to save it for the people. The failure to please the growers and to carry on successfully wore on him until his heart began to give him serious problems.

He was in San Francisco at the time of the 1906 earthquake and fire and escaped without injury. He managed to get back to Fresno and then left shortly after for a trip to the Baths in Germany. He died aboard the ship before he reached Europe on May 27 at the age of sixty-four.

When all was said and done, when Kearney died the people had the surprise of their lives: he left his land, money, and possessions to the University of California for educational affairs. In the course of time, the lovely park was again used for the people of Fresno County. For the foreseeable future, it will be there as a reminder of this man who contributed to building up early agricultural Fresno.

Kearney's three-story sun-dried brick adobe dwelling was built in 1900. The house, previously called the "Residence," was beautifully furnished in fine Victorian. Today, the building is often called the "Mansion," though by today's standards it is more of a fine house. (S. Bybyk)

Legacy

Kearney built a beautiful scenic drive from the edge of Fresno to his estate. When it was finished at the cost of many thousands of dollars, he deeded it to the county, but kept up the maintenance as long as he lived. The attractive tree-lined drive that leads out to the park is now reaching a historic status. Towering palms, eucalyptus trees, and oleander bushes make it a shady, pleasant drive that was once called "Chateau Fresno Drive" but is now known as Kearney Avenue.

He established a magnificent estate on his seven thousand acres. It was well-planned and a great success in every phase of farm life. It practically became a small town. He built up a 240-acre park that was probably the finest in California at the time. It was laid out by a professional landscape engineer. Every species of rose known then was planted; they were terraced to give the look of knolls, to take away the long flat aspect of the plains.

He bought exotic plants and shrubs in Europe and had them sent to Fresno to be planted in the park. Fruit trees were set out and lived to bear fruit, which sold for profit. Thousands upon thousands of trees were planted—from forest trees to ornamentals. Shady, restful drives led through winding terrain. A teahouse was constructed as a recreation center for the employees and townspeople.

The beautiful grounds that still grace the land that Kearney called home serve as a public park, and the mansion is the shrine to the Victorian era. The park was once considered the most fabulous one in the West.

His beautiful Kearney Mansion continues under the stewardship of the Fresno County Historical Society as a museum and base for historical research and preservation.

Epilogue

To my dear readers, I want to express my deep appreciation of your interest in the stories of our county's past.

People make history. It comes to us in many ways. In some instances and areas, it comes from sections of country that have been uninhabited or hostile to humans through time and history.

The history of an area may first be seen in symbols written on stone, or by ridged terrain in a badlands country. It may be learned from the strata of the soils along dry lakes and riverbeds. It may come from fossils and bones or from footprints and tracks.

In the course of time there comes proof of the habitation of man. Shelters appear, a tumble of ruins, perhaps—true signs of life. One may live for a certain length of time in the forages of the elements, but eventually, the light descends, and a hut is fashioned. It has walls and a roof, which is much better than living in a cave or a brush lair. And so wildernesses give way to the coming and demands of man.

It was thus that history has been recounted in our country. While this book focuses on modern history, the early history of people in the region goes back up to thirteen thousand years with the Miwok and Yokuts peoples. Since the area was colonized relatively recently by settlers on behalf of the US, this county's history goes back to the early mining days on the banks of the great old San Joaquin River, a powerful energy for all time.

Change

Then came the buildings that replaced the campsites. The little settlement of Rootville expanded. The military came to protect the settlers from the Indigenous peoples who had previously lived in the region, and gave a name to the pioneer spot. The village grew, reaching a town's estate.

As the westward trek marched on, the miners along the river sighed their regrets and took up the life of civilization. A county was born, and the village became the county seat.

Millerton had its days of glory. More people remained than went by, for it was a bonny spot tucked there against the great boulders and rocks that guarded the transition of time and tide in men's affairs. The sun shone clear and bright for much of the year, but there were hazards, too, when Old Man River often went on a rampage.

Fruitful Soil

The hill soil proved fruitful, and gold was soon no longer the economic focus of the region. Experiments produced vegetables, fruit, and grain. It could be called a fair land.

When it was a county seat it teemed with life, but it was, after all, far out on the lonely reaches of the fast-growing state. The newcomers who had brought with them much of their own past from other areas became bolder as the railroad whistled through the once dreary plains land and the locomotives chugged in with the news of better things to come.

The great plains proved to be a garden of Eden, the lonely vistas giving way to a new type of civilization. Today our City of Fresno that came in with a train whistle continues as a great city.

Old-timers Go

The old-timers of the county have vanished year by year. Their descendants are now the power of history. Some of the richness of Fresno's past will go with them. Do help to garner what they can offer before they take it with them into the limbo of memory.

I would like to charge you to preserve all that is rich with years, and that you take seriously the preserving of history.

This can be done partially by passing on the antiques of other eras for preservation. You can also revere the objects of your generation and preserve the stories of life as you live it, for that, too, will be history someday. Do this by writing your family histories, the stories of your ancestors, and your own.

Reach back into your memories and your parents' memories. Garner the years as best you can. There may be elements of rich history in your own background.

It has been a pleasure to have reached into the county's archives and given you some part of the vanished days of history.

Dearth of History

I speak the truth when I say there is a dearth of history in this county. It is broad and spacious and human, but little-by-little, time takes the past further from our reach. Our librarians try to seek it out. They want to pass it on to you.

The public librarians and the librarians of the historical societies are generous with their time and interest.

The board members of the Fresno County Historical Society and the volunteer workers are leaders to whom you can look to preserve your history. They will go to great lengths to help you garner and preserve essential things of history.

I cannot let loose of the happy strings that have bound us without this word of farewell, to you, my readers. We have traveled into the past together with what information I could glean. There have been so many of you who have helped me document our county's rich past. You may not have realized how much. Your messages to me by note or card, by telephone, by a chat at a social gathering, or on the street, have been so generous, and I have loved you for it.

I go to other fields of endeavor, leaving wonderful memories here. I have had a nice life in Fresno that has been molded greatly by the work of love that history can become.

And now, as I've closed so many pieces over the years, it's...

THIRTY.

Acknowledgements

Grateful acknowledgements are extended to the many who have shared their interest in and information of Fresno County lore in helping to bring this volume to the public. Some of this information has come in casual conversation with old-timers and historically minded folks. Fresno historians have added their wealth of knowledge, and libraries and librarians have aided in supplying facts and dates.

Both old and recent newspapers and magazines have played a part in the gathering of information for the compilation of "Fresno's Past."

Fresno County Historical Society

Most notable is the role that the Fresno County Historical Society played in creating this manuscript.

Edwin M. Eaton, president of the Society, has a deep and intense interest in history. He is a native son of California, and a native Fresnan as well. He is the son of Louis Einstein, a prominent businessman and banker of the early days.

The Society staff members include Elvin Bell, James W. Canfield, Richard E. Denton, Edwin M. Eaton, Mrs. Darrow English, Julia Harris

Hays, Mrs. Irene D. Lahl, William J. Mortland, Jr., A. B. Olson, Mrs. Erma Peirson, Dan R. Pollard, Emory Ratcliffe, Fred L. Swartz, I. H. Tielman, and Raymund F. Wood.

Mrs. Lahl, the secretary for society, did not grow up in the state or county, but she does have a great sense of history. She hails from Connecticut.

Julia Harris Hays, the treasurer, comes from a Fresno pioneer family. Her parents were Amazon Showl Hays and Martha King Harris Hays. They were both Southerners. Miss Hays attended the Ranson and Bridges Finishing School for Girls at Piedmont and has lived all her life in Fresno.

Raymund F. Wood, of the library staff at Fresno State College, is the program chairman and editor of the quarterly bulletin, "Fresno, Past and Present," of the society. A historian in his own right, he contributes a bit of history to each issue of the bulletin.

Executive Board Member Historians

There are several executive board members who do not hold a special duty office in the Fresno County Historical Society but contribute from their spot on the staff. They are men of action, with fine civic and county backgrounds, each with an avowed interest in historical matters. Their combined talents, skills, and interests give the society a fine basis for operation.

Richard E. Denton is vice president of the Historical Society. He has been a resident of the area for almost forty years, coming to the county in 1925. Five years later he became interested in the Society. He has been a member of the executive board for many years. Mr. Denton majored in history in college and followed up his interest in later years, traveling a great deal. He has had a special interest in visiting national parks and followed a public relations career until his retirement. He became well known through his interest in and addresses on the subject of eucalyptus trees. He has served on the Board of Trustees of Storyland and with the Fresno Executive Club.

Professor Emory Ratcliffe is a charter member of the Fresno County Historical Society. He served on the Old War History Committee and assisted in establishing the Society forty-five years ago. He has always held a spot in the Society and has served as president, secretary, and historian. He is professor emeritus of Fresno State College, where he taught history and political science.

The Librarians

Mrs. June English is the head librarian for the Fresno County Historical Society. She is a very dedicated worker and spends all her free time in the library room assigned for the housing of the society's historical records. These records take many forms. They come in newspapers, clipping files, old letters, diaries and family histories, books, pictures, registers, maps, biographies, documents, charts and legal papers, inventions and contracts.

The above is only a part of the library work. Mrs. English takes off with her own tape recorder whenever she hears of someone with a historical background. She helps in booths at fairs, carrying Fresno County's past with exhibits and talk.

Mrs. English has an inherent love of history and is well read. Having lived "all over the West" as she puts it, the first thing she does when she finds herself in a new area is to learn all about its history.

I also want to take this opportunity to thank the reference librarians of the city for their great understanding of the needs and the perplexities of researchers. These fine people have done so much to help uncover the city's and the county's former years. I am especially indebted to the reference division at Central Library and the librarians at Gillis and North Fresno Branches. To each individual, my thanks!

The Fresno Guide

Without *The Fresno Guide* granting me the weekly column that ran on Thursdays from mid-1963 to the beginning of 1965, I would not have had the motivation and ability to eventually create this book, *Fresno's Past*.

Erma Peirson, 1965

About the Author

Erma Patterson was born in Missouri 1891 and spent her childhood there.

After high school, she got her first job working for the Republican, a local newspaper in Aurora, Nebraska, while she attended a teacher's college. After her graduation from college in 1910, she taught in elementary schools across five different states: Nebraska, Colorado, Wyoming, California, and Nevada.

With the First World War underway, Erma decided to pen and publish some patriotic songs to support the war effort. She wrote a "Poem Song" and sent it to a music company in Chicago. They hired a musician to write the accompanying music. She submitted many titles for review and would have to pay the musician. In 1919, she got copyrights for three songs, "Our Uncle Sammy," "The Star of Gold," and "We Made the Kaiser Rally to Red, White and Blue."

Erma married Wilfred "Bill" Robinson Peirson in 1922 in Walnut Creek, California when she was thirty-one. Shortly afterward, they moved to Madera, California. For a year, she was a reporter and feature writer for the Madera Mercury news. She got a full-time position with the County as Secretary to the Horticultural Commissioner.

In September 1928 during the economic depression, Erma was pregnant and moved with her husband and three-year old son to Colombia, South America for a job he was offered there in the oil industry. They lived in Barrancabermeja for just over a year. When she became pregnant with their third child, they moved back to California because there was concern about the pregnancy.

Although her primary focus was on raising their three children, Erma enjoyed writing. She had articles published in *Boys' Life* and *Progress* magazines.

They eventually moved to Barstow, where Erma developed a love for the desert. She would travel up and down the communities and towns along the Mojave River and talk to the older people who lived there to document their stories about the area and the river.

When the family moved to China Lake, Erma worked as associate editor and then editor of the *Rocketeer* from 1945 to 1950. While there, she wrote a column called Desert Spotlight, a collection of 250 desert stories under the title, Desert Scrapbook, and a series called Death Valley Lore.

Erma attributed her interest in writing a desert book to desert author Major George Palmer Putman, the husband of Amelia Earhart. He had remarried after Amelia's death and was living in Mount Whitney Portals, north of China Lake. She had an interview with him for the *Rocketeer* and he discovered her interest in the desert. He told her, "Mrs. Peirson, promise me something. Stay with the desert. You write so well."

In 1956, Erma wrote *The Kern's Desert*, which was published by the Kern County Historical Society. It was the first book she officially published and was well received. She also wrote short stories about desert life, both nonfiction and from her own experiences.

Erma enrolled in the local college in the fall of 1957. At the age of sixty-seven, she had the distinction of being the oldest member of the graduating class of 1958 when she received her degree in General Education at Fresno City College.

Erma had the distinction of being a member of the Fresno County Historical Society. In 1959, she even became a member of the Board of Directors. In the newspaper, *The Fresno Guide*, Erma had a weekly column called Fresno's Past from 1963 to 1965. She planned to make this column into her next book, but she was not able to finish the project prior to her passing.

Erma became a widow in 1963 with her husband Bill's passing. She moved to Apple Valley in 1965 and became the editor of the *Apple Valley Bonanza*, writing weekly articles. She had one series called Apple Valley Golden Land. She also wrote a column for the *Hesperia Resorter* called Desert Drama.

She published her book *The Mojave River and Its Valley* in 1970. It was highly regarded and was the culmination of her life's work. The town of Apple Valley declared July 31, 1970 as Erma Peirson Day in recognition of her efforts and her love for the desert.

Erma passed away July 21, 1971 at the age of eighty, following a heart attack. To honor her work, her grandson, Robert Peirson, compiled, edited, and published her Fresno's Past work posthumously in 2024.

Erma Peirson, Author of **Fresno's Past** (S. Bybyk)

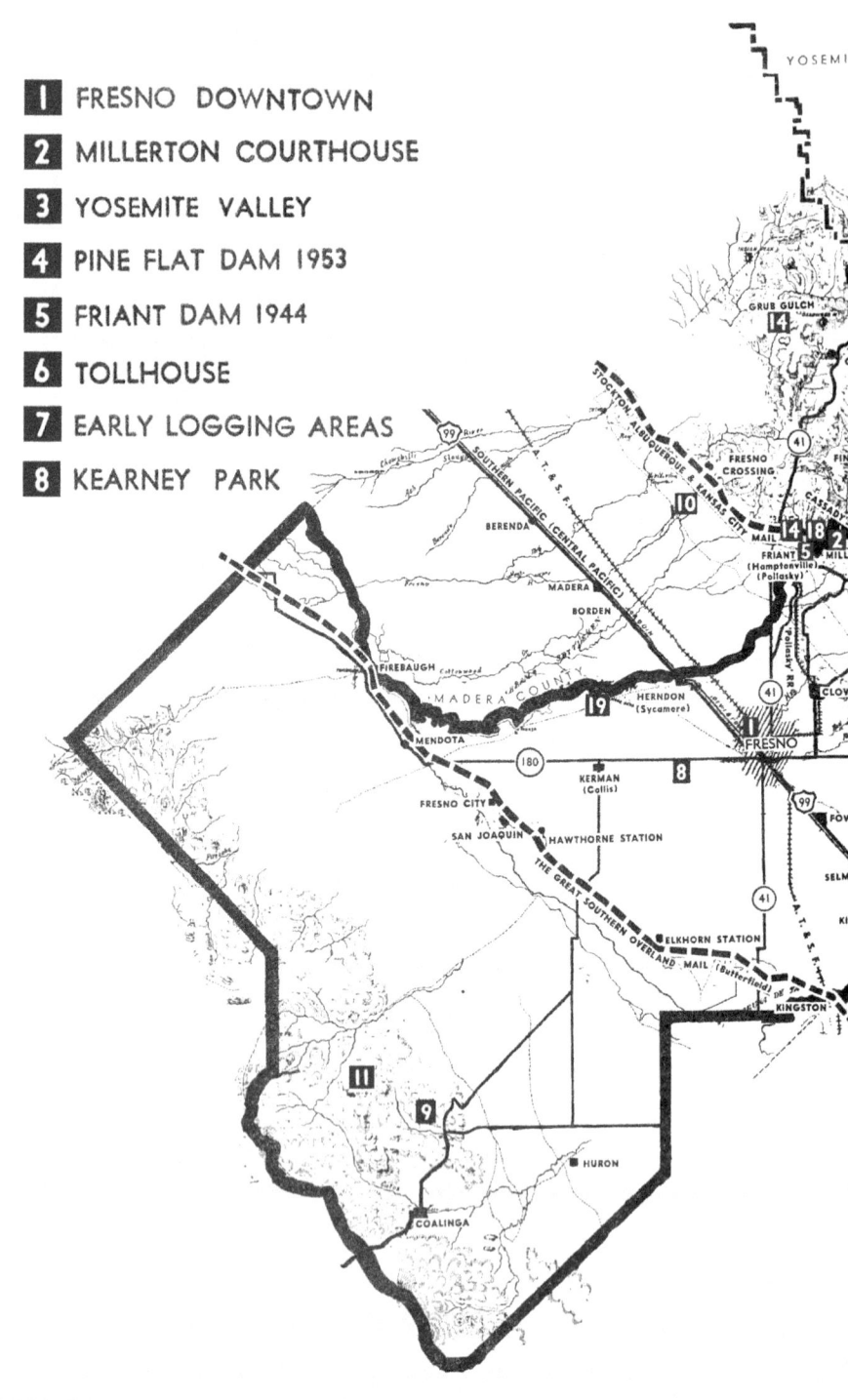

1. FRESNO DOWNTOWN
2. MILLERTON COURTHOUSE
3. YOSEMITE VALLEY
4. PINE FLAT DAM 1953
5. FRIANT DAM 1944
6. TOLLHOUSE
7. EARLY LOGGING AREAS
8. KEARNEY PARK

9 OIL-Discovered 1864	**15** MORO ROCK
10 SAVAGE MONUMENT	**16** SIERRA REDWOODS
11 MURIETA ROCKS	**17** TEHIPITE DOME
12 KINGS RIVER CANYON	**18** FORT MILLER
13 DEVIL'S POST PILE	**19** SYCAMORE POINT
14 GOLD DIGGING	**20** MUIR TRAIL